STALAG ASSAULT

Recent Titles by Leo Kessler from Severn House

Writing as Leo Kessler

S.S. Wotan Series
Assault On Baghdad
The Bormann Mission
Breakout from Stalingrad
Death's Eagles
Death from the Arctic Sky
Operation Fury
Operation Long Jump
The Hitler Werewolf Murders
S S Attacks
Stalag Assault
Wotan Missions

The Churchill Papers
Patton's Wall

Writing as Duncan Harding

Assault on St Nazaire
Attack New York!
Operation Judgement
Sink the Ark Royal
Sink the Graf Spee
Sink the Prince of Wales
Sink the Tirpitz
The Tobruk Rescue

Writing as Charles Whiting

The Common Smith VC Series
The Baltic Run
In Turkish Waters
Death on the Rhine
Hell's Angels
The Japanese Princess
Passage to Petrograd

Non-Fiction
Paths of Death and Glory

STALAG ASSAULT

Leo Kessler

This first world edition published in Great Britain 2000 by
SEVERN HOUSE PUBLISHERS LTD of
9–15 High Street, Sutton, Surrey SM1 1DF.
This first world edition published in the U.S.A. 2000 by
SEVERN HOUSE PUBLISHERS INC of
595 Madison Avenue, New York, N.Y. 10022.

British Library Cataloguing in Publication Data

Kessler, Leo, 1926-
The stalag assault. - (S.S. Wotan series)
1.World War, 1939-1945 - Campaigns - Fiction
2.War stories
I. Title
823.9'14 [F]

ISBN 0-7278-5538-7

Typeset by Palimpsest Book Production Ltd.
Polmont, Stirlingshire, Scotland.
Printed and bound in Great Britain by
MPG Books Ltd, Bodmin, Cornwall.

PART ONE

A Rescue is Proposed

One

"Holy Mother of God!"

Horowitz's curse broke the sudden echoing silence. The pain stabbed his foot like a thrust from a sizzling, red-hot poker. Abruptly he felt sick. "Don't," he commanded himself through gritted teeth. "That's a frigging enough. Don't cough up ya cookies!"

Up front the thick grey smoke was clearing. The ambush had ended. Now the shooting was over. Horowitz could see the running crouched figures of the enemy, heading to the smoking burning convoy, dead, charred Americans lying in scorched steaming snow on both sides of the track. They were in white camouflaged overalls. All of them wore white hoods, too. That's why the leading scouts of the 'All Americans' hadn't seen them lying in ambush until it had been too damned late. "What a frigging mess," Horowitz moaned, trying to fight off the hot tears of pain and despair.

An enormous Tiger tank was rumbling out of the forest. It snapped the pines like matchsticks. Behind it it threw up a whirling white wake of flying snow. Still he could see the black-and-white Maltese cross on its steel hide clearly. Horowitz groaned again. This time it wasn't from the pain in his foot. It was from anger. The Krauts had caught them with their drawers down, that was for sure. Now they – *he* – were for it.

He flashed a glance down at his wounded foot as he sprawled there in the snow-filled ditch. The slug had burst open his brown jump boot. Blood was spurting through a ragged hole in the leather in a bright red arc. He cursed.

"How in the Sam Hill am I gonna get out of this frigging mess with a crocked up foot?" He hardly recognised his own voice as he said the words.

Desperately he looked up at the grey, lowering winter sky, flecked here and there with drifting patches of brown smoke, as if he were half-expecting an answer from heaven. But on this cruel December morning in the embattled Belgian Ardennes, God was looking the other way. He cursed again.

Now the 60-ton Tiger had ground to a halt in a flurry of snow. Panzer grenadiers sprang hastily from its metal deck. Brigadier Horowitz knew why. The Kraut kids were eager to loot the shot-up US column before their white-clad comrades got there. They'd be after the Hershey bars and Camels. Christ on a crutch, he told himself, they were little better than schoolkids, running through the ankle-deep snow. But cruel little jerks all the same, he added. Frigging well kill yer for a pack of smokes.

Then he forgot the kids of the *Waffen SS*. He pressed his right hand down on the wound – hard. He had to stop the bleeding as quickly as possible. Awkwardly, with his left hand, he started to pull the general's stars from his collar. He tugged off his helmet, also adorned with a single star. He threw it into the snow-heavy bushes, gasping now with the effort and the electrically stabbing pain in his ankle. Now he was sweating like a pig despite the intense cold.

Up ahead around the 'deuce-and-a-half' truck, a giant of an SS man had bitten off the neck of a bottle of what looked like bourbon and was swilling it down his throat greedily, his Adam's apple going up and down his neck like an express elevator. "Lucky, greedy bastard," he murmured to himself as he completed pulling off the rest of his general's insignia. At this particular moment he felt he could sell his own white-haired momma for a stiff shot of rye.

Up front Sergeant Schulze gasped and wiped a dirty paw across his thick, wet lips and announced to no one in particular, "Heaven, arse and cloudburst, that hit the spot."

Next to him Corporal Matz, his long-time running mate in SS Assault Regiment 'Wotan', said plaintively, eyeing the bottle the giant held anxiously, "Damn yer glassy orbits, Schulzi, save a drop for yer old comrade for pity's sake, *Kumpel.*"

Schulze raised his massive left haunch and let rip with one of his not unmusical farts – indeed the huge SS NCO was celebrated throughout the whole of the *Waffen SS* for the quality of his farts. There was even a rumour that the Führer had once promised him a medal – Cultural Order, Second Class – on account of their sheer musical beauty, which he had apparently compared with certain passages in Wagner. However, malicious and envious high-ranking officers in Himmler's HQ had vetoed the award. "Take a ride on that, old house," Schulze said happily.

Matz's wrinkled, monkey-like face blanched and his eyes watered. "Great crap on the Christmas Tree," he choked appalled. "That sort of thing is . . . is nothing else but a crime against humanity, Schulzi!"

Sergeant Schulze ignored the comment. "All right," he snapped, "get those cardboard soldiers of yours searching the rest of these trucks. Collar any Amis" – he meant Americans – "who haven't croaked. The CO'll need 'em for interrogation." He looked around the snow-heavy firs of the Ardennes forest. "And then let's do a bunk tootsweet. This place gives me the creeps. *Beweg' Dich, Arsch mit Ohren!*"

'The Arse-with-Ears' moved. Together, with a handful of the young panzer grenadiers, he moved forward purposefully, Schmeisser machine pistol clutched at the ready, while Schulze leaned against the wrecked truck, watching with narrowed eyes. Matz and he had been together since the start. He wasn't going to lose him now to some yellow-arsed *jiddisch* sniper from America – the 'Land of Unbound Possibilities'.

Horowitz saw them coming. His good hand flashed to his Colt. Then he thought better of it. He didn't stand a chance against half a company of young Krauts. Still he knew he had to get away – and get away fast. If the Krauts took him prisoner and then figured out he was a general officer, they'd soon put the squeeze on him for information and, knowing the reputation of the SS, they'd soon have him frigging chirping away like a frigging yellow canary bird. Hadn't they shot 150 GIs in cold blood after they had surrendered at Malmedy only a week ago?*

He forgot that unpleasant thought as quickly as it had come. Instead he drew the Colt and hid it in his waistband for a quick draw. He opened the leather flap of his holster as if he had already gotten rid of the big forty-five. Just like the bastards of the SS, he could play dirty tricks, too.

Up ahead the SS had paused near a truck with a ruptured radiator and with both its front tyres shot to ribbons. Thin white smoke rose from its bullet-riddled engine. The Krauts had spotted something. It was his chance. He rose to his feet, holding on to the skeletal branches and wished next moment he hadn't. Pain surged through his leg right up to the hip. It was worse than the gut shot he had suffered at Ste-Mère-Eglise on D-Day. Still he hung on, gasping for breath as if he had just run a great race.

The SS were still halted. He could hear them talking among themselves. Their voices were calm and conversational, as if they had all the frigging time in the world; as if there wasn't an American within a mile or so. Bitterly he told himself perhaps they were right. At this particular moment, it seemed as if the whole US Army in Belgium had bugged out and left him on his lonesome.

General Horowitz dismissed the thought. He moved on painfully. With one hand he pulled himself from branch to branch. With the other he fumbled with the grenade attached to the webbing on his chest. He tugged off the tape with his finger and thumb. It kept the detonator in place. In the last resort he'd use it, he knew that. Not against the Krauts, but

* The infamous 'Malmedy Massacre' of December 17, 1944.

for himself. It was his duty to do so. He couldn't fall into their hands with what he knew. He crawled on.

Schulze turned the dead American over with the toe of his big boot. Like all of them he had been brutalised by war. You never dirtied your hands on a stiff, if you could help it; you always used your boot. "Staff officer," he commented, looking down at those sightless eyes set in a white intelligent face. "Look at them flippers of his. Ain't done a day's *marlokking* in all his born days." Like all the 'old hares', as the veterans called themselves, he used the Russian word for work. It was a common habit of theirs. They had been in the East so long, they used Russian all the time.

"So, what's it mean?" Matz asked and wondered if it was worth attempting to loot the dead man. He was awful bloody. His ripped-open chest looked as if someone had thrown a handful of strawberry jam at it.

Schulze shrugged carelessly. "Do I walk across the shitting water, ape-turd? How in three devils' name am I supposed to know, eh?"

Matz wasn't offended. He had known Schulzi too long to be hurt even by the big man's most offensive statements. "Don't rupture yersen," he said quite mildly.

"Go and piss in the wind—" Schulze began and then stopped in mid-sentence as he recognised the lean, trim officer with his battered peaked cap tilted at its usual rakish angle. "It's the CO," he snapped, straightening. "Get the lead outa yer hairy ass."

Obersturmbannführer von Dodenburg's harshly handsome face broke into a taut grin when he saw the two old hares. "Looting again, I see, you big rogue," he said to Schulze, his keen icy blue eyes taking in the scene – the smoking trucks, the dead to both sides of the forest trail like bundles of abandoned khaki rags, the nearest Ami with what looked like a gray snake slithered out of the red maw of his shattered guts, his pockets standing up and empty as they had been rifled.

"Just a few souvenirs for the folks back home, sir," Schulze answered.

Kuno von Dodenburg gave the big man a knowing smile. "The only kind of souvenirs *you* return home with, Schulze, are the ones that end up with the – er – lady in question having to go and see the pox doctor."

Matz nudged his running mate gleefully. "See, the CO knows yer, you big fart-cannon. Souvenirs . . . pox doctors. He's got you nailed—" He stopped short abruptly. The CO was no longer looking at them. Instinctively his hand dropped to his own weapon, as von Dodenburg bent his knees into a fighting crouch, blue eyes fixed on some spot to their rear.

"What is it?" Schulze hissed urgently. "What d'yer see?"

Von Dodenburg didn't answer. But now he knew his eyes weren't fooling him. There was something up there and it had to be an Ami! His right forefinger began to curl around the trigger of his machine pistol in white-knuckled tension.

Horowitz bit his bottom lip till the blood came and filled his mouth, hot and coppery. His tortured dark face was lathered with sweat like a film of Vaseline. Fire and pain racked his tortured body. Step by step, each move achieved by effort of sheer naked will-power. Now the first pines of the thick Belgian forest were only a matter of feet away. He could see the pointed hoof marks of the deer leading to it and safety quite clearly. Move it, he urged himself onwards, feeling the energy drain from him, as if someone had opened an unseen tap. Again that harsh little voice at the back of his brain urged him on. 'Only another few seconds . . . keep moving . . . you're nearly there . . . Come on you soft bag o' crap . . . *Move!*'

Suddenly, startlingly, the challenge rang out, echoing and re-echoing in the surrounding circle of hills, "*Halt . . . stehenbleiben . . . oder ich schiesse . . .*" Then in accented but recognisable English: "Stop . . . no move . . . or I shoot!"

The challenge stabbed Horowitz like the razor-sharp blade of a knife being slid into his guts. He hesitated. What was he to do? He looked at the edge of the forest, with the pines, their boughs heavy and sparkling with the new snow. For an instant he had a vision of a childhood Christmas in New England: snow, peace, happiness, joy. Then he remembered where he was and the hope drained from his body. He reached up, forgetting the pain, the pure white of the snow at his feet swiftly turning a dull red from his wound. He grunted. With one and the same movement he pulled out the cotter pin of the grenade, and raised the deadly little weapon above his head.

Schulze was the first to spot the move. "Watch out, he's got a grenade!" he bellowed fervently.

"*Voller Deckung!*" Matz yelled.

The young grenadiers needed no urging. They flung themselves to the ground. Von Dodenburg raised his Schmeisser. He didn't seem to take aim. There was no need to. The range was so short. Under other circumstances he would have aimed at the Ami's back, the broadest and easiest target. This time something stopped him. Instead he ripped a burst just about where the enemy was beginning to throw the grenade.

Horowitz yelped with pain. It seemed as if someone had struck his right arm a tremendous blow with an iron bar. The grenade flew from his clutch. He had been in combat long enough to duck instinctively. Next moment the earth erupted a a couple of yards away. A burst of searing orange flame. A wave of blast slapped him across the face. His breath was dragged from his lungs, leaving him panting and gasping for air like some ancient asthmatic in the throes of an attack. Next instant a red mist descended upon him and he knew no more.

Von Dodenburg stared at the helmet with its lone gold star. He knew what the latter signified. It was the helmet of a one-star general. He frowned suddenly, puzzled. The dead GIs were all too young to be a general. Paras attained that exalted rank earlier than poor hairy-assed stubble hoppers

– he meant infantry – like themselves. But even in the parachute troopers, twenty-year-olds didn't become generals. His frown deepened. Where was the general? Had he escaped? He opened his mouth to say something to Schulze, but he never managed it.

The first Thunderbolt was falling out of the sky in a silver fury, its engine going all out, machine guns chattering angrily. "*Jabos* . . . fighter bombers," the air lookout cried, even as the first salvo of tracer bullets ripped his skinny chest apart. Next moment there was another zipping across the valley at tree-top height, its prop wash lashing the pine fronds to and fro crazily and the men of SS Assault Regiment Wotan were running for their lives. Behind them they left the dead, already beginning to stiffen in the murderous snow, with the first gentle snowflakes starting to drift down. By nightfall they would have covered the corpses and no one would ever know what had happened here . . .

Two

"WAR OVER BY NEW YEAR – OFFICIAL!" the old news vendor yelled without conviction as they came into Shaftesbury Avenue. He thrust a copy of the *Daily Express* at the hawkfaced naval officer huddled in the back of the Humber staff car in his 'British warm'. Lt Commander Mallory shook his head. Like the old newspaper salesman he didn't believe the official release one bit. Over the Channel, the Allies and the Germans were fighting out a ding-dong battle in the Belgian Ardennes. And on this late December day, it looked almost as if the Huns were winning.

"It's a nice thought anyway," he said to himself half aloud. Like most lonely men he talked to himself quite often. Up front the pretty Wren driver said, "Won't be half a mo, sir. The special constable'll let us through in a brace of shakes, sir."

Mallory grunted his thanks. He looked out of the window, mind racing on why he had been called back from the Continent to meet C. It had been months now since he had seen the poker-faced, ancient head of the British Secret Service. He stared at the London crowd. They looked particularly grey and war weary this snowy December day. Poor sods, he thought, they've had enough – nearly six years of war. 'Bout time it was all bloody well over.

The elderly special constable in his white-painted helmet had just signalled the Wren driver could move off again when the sirens began to sound their stomach-churning howl once more. Hurriedly he waved the Humber to the kerb. The Wren obliged, muttering a very unladylike curse. Mallory tut-tutted as the constable came across, saluting when he saw the tarnished gold braid on Mallory's battered old sea-going cap. "The handbrake on, sir . . . Windows open on account of the blast – and into that doorway yonder. No time for the shelters, sir."

Mallory moaned. "Must we go, constable? I'm in a deuce of a hurry."

The old policeman managed to raise a weary smile. His eyes were watery and his ashen face looked pinched. He might well be dying. "To the boneyard, sir? Them doodlebugs are real buggers. If yer'll pardon my French, miss," he added for the sake of the pretty Wren.

Mallory got the point. He nodded. He watched as the driver swung her elegant, black-clad legs out of the driver's seat. The stockings were sheer silk and non-regulation, as he noted with a sudden thickening of his loins. Her knickers, too. He grinned in that sardonic manner of his. His Marauders wouldn't have objected to having 'a slice o' that lovely grub,' as they would have put it gleefully. But then neither would he, he told himself, as he followed the other two into the nearest doorway.

A sudden tense stillness fell over the London street. All traffic had ceased. The chatter of the pedestrians, too. Even Mallory, hardened veteran as he was, felt the tension. Then there it was. The small hairs at the back of his head stood erect. He felt a cold finger of fear trace its way down the small of his back. It was the inevitability of the bloody thing up there, he told himself. To the east it was visible now. The new German 'revenge' weapon, the V-1, chugging away like the old two-stroke motor bike that he had used in his last year at Eton before he was expelled on account of that unfortunate business with a beak's wife.

Now the ack-ack took up the challenge. Shaftesbury Avenue reverberated and echoed. Red and yellow balls of flame exploded in the grey sky. Grey smoke streaked the heavens. Still the pilotless plane, carrying a ton of high explosive, came on purposefully.

Next to him the young Wren pressed herself close.

Through the thick uniform he could sense her soft flesh and smell her odour of cheap scent and female body. He tugged at his left eye-patch a little uncertainly. "Rotten sodding Jerry bastard," the old Special cursed to no one in particular. At any other time, Mallory would have grinned. But not now. The situation was too serious. As soon as the doodlebug engine cut out and it fell out of the sky at 400 mph, people were going to die – innocent men, women and kids.

Abruptly the thunder of the anti-aircraft guns stopped. They tensed. This was it. From the west one of the new clipped-wing Spitfires came zooming in. It streaked across the sky at a tremendous rate. Time and time again it disappeared into grey puffballs of smoke only to reappear an instant later, going all out, heading straight for the pilotless plane. "My God," Mallory gasped in admiration, "that RAF type's got some bloody nerve."

"He's going to deflect the wing, sir," the Wren said, voice shaky. "Deflect it off course and away from the city."

The two planes came closer and closer. Below, thousands of Londoners, the danger forgotten now, craned their necks to watch this strange duel between man and machine. Now the Spitfire was flying almost parallel with the V-1. Next to him, the Wren held her breath and for one frightening moment Mallory thought her heart might have stopped with the shock. "Here she goes," he cried, his hands clenched into claws dripping with sweat so that it hurt. "Get the bugger!"

With a sudden half-roll the Spitfire turned into the doodlebug. Abruptly the V-1's engine cut out. Her nose tipped downwards. The Spitfire pilot nudged the pilotless plane. But it was too late. He couldn't deflect the V-1 from her course. The plane fell out of the sky, as the Spitfire pilot broke off to the left before it was too late.

"Open yer gobs!" the special constable yelled above the snarl and roar of the Spitfire's engine going all over. "Don't want yer eardrums to b—" The rest of his urgent warning was drowned by a tremendous, all-consuming explosion. A great wind roared down Shaftesbury Avenue. The tall buildings on either side shook and trembled like stage properties. A house collapsed. The windscreen of the Humber staff car cracked into a glittering spider's web of broken glass. Glass cascaded down on the three sheltering in the doorway. The Wren screamed with fear, her uniform lashed against her plump body by the blast. Opposite, greedy yellow flames were beginning to lick the facade of a music shop. In an instant all was chaos.

As far off the ambulances began to jingle urgently, Mallory raised the Wren gently from her crouched position. She was shaking. "It's all right now," he said quietly. The sirens were now beginning to sound the all clear. The emergency was over for the time being. But Mallory knew that the 'buzzbombs', as the Yanks called them – he remembered that they would be playing a role in what was soon to come, would be back. They always were. "When we get to our destination, I'll buy you a pink gin – *a large one*." He smiled at her encouragingly.

Wanly she responded and told herself that despite the lieutenant-commander's tough forbidding appearance with his black eye-patch and livid purple scar running down the side of his hard, lean face, he seemed a kind man, concerned about others – and these days there were not many active-service naval officers who were like that. "Thank you, sir," she began. Then her hand flew to the side of her pretty face and the words died on her pale lips. "*Look*," she said in a faint tremulous voice.

The other two followed the direction of her gaze.

A head lay in the centre of a debris-littered Shaftesbury Avenue. It was complete with worn, cheap cloth cap. A few feet away lay the body of its former owner, crumpled into the gretesque position of the violently done to death. It was the old newspaper vendor, the scrawled legend, "WAR OVER BY NEW YEAR – OFFICIAL!" mocking him in death.

In silence the two of them crunched their way back to the

Humber across the broken glass. Behind them the old special constable adjusted his white helmet and said to no one in particular, "What a bloody 'orrible war." Lt Commander Mallory couldn't have agreed with him more.

White's was packed. Now the air-raid sirens had sounded the all clear, the civil service civilians in their high-winged collars and striped trousers and the middle-aged, red-tabbed senior officers were coming out of the air-raid shelters and heading for the Club's bar for a stiff drink before they returned to their offices. Everywhere men with plummy voices were demanding, "A double, steward . . . Pimm's please" . . . "I say, make that a double, will you?"

Mallory looked around him with a certain amount of disdain. They were all so self-important, he told himself, full of themselves. All the same he knew these civil servants and brass hats had their uses; they kept the country running. Besides he had been born into their class and indeed he was an occasional member of the self-same club. All the same . . . He didn't finish the thought. Instead he concentrated on getting himself a drink, just as he had just done for the shocked Wren down below in the entrance. He knew by the way she had looked up at him, eyes full of gratitude and admiration, she would have been a pushover for tonight. But somehow, he felt he wouldn't be spending the night in the Big Smoke – with or without female company.

For a minute or two, he sipped his drink, the sound all around him receding into a hushed distance, as he considered the haste in which he had submitted his report on Holland and been summoned here – there had been hardly time to distribute the contents of the looted Germany paymaster's strongbox and get them settled in Brussels before he was on his way to London. Not that his Marauders minded. As ex-barrow boy Stevens had confided in him just before he'd left, "Don't worry about us, guv. My guess is that most of yer Marauders won't be knowing no pain for next seventy-two hours." He had winked in that cunning, knowing cockney manner of his. "If you take my meaning?"

Mallory had. It'd be wine, women and song – and not too much of the song – for his bunch of jailbirds for the next three days. Inwardly he sighed at the thought of the trouble the Marauders would undoubtedly get themselves into in the next few days. He could see himself squaring the local provost marshal as usual and greasing the palms of several battered Belgian gendarmes. Then he dismissed the thought of his men. He had just spotted the man he had crossed the Channel so hurriedly to see.

He was a skinny, pale-faced older man with thinning grey hair, dressed in a grey suit. Indeed everything seemed grey about him, as if he had just emerged from a long stay in a dust-filled cupboard – or grave, the harsh voice at the back of his brain corrected him. The only splash of colour was the man's Eton tie.

For a moment or two Mallory studied the man, who officially didn't exist, head of a powerful organisation, which, too, officially didn't exist either. Surprisingly enough, despite the press of important people all around him, he and his companion had plenty of room. No one seemed to be prepared to infringe on the grey man's privacy; and Mallory knew why. He was looking at the man who directed that savage secret war in the shadows, where men of all nationalities died suddenly, brutally and for no apparent reason. C was a very powerful man indeed. Even Churchill listened to him.

Mallory finished his drink, cleared his throat, tugged at his shabby naval tunic adorned with the fading ribbons of the DSO and DSC and walked over. His eyes met the faded ones of the old grey man in the mirror behind the bar. The latter nodded slightly. It was the indication that he could approach closer. Mallory did so.

C put down his glass of sherry and said in a low dry voice, "Good of you to come, Mallory." He didn't offer his hand or to buy the newcomer a drink. Instead he frowned at his younger companion. Hastily the latter drained his glass and without another word departed.

C waited till his companion was out of earshot and said, "Best of all places to meet, Mallory." It was as if he were answering some unspoken question that Mallory had just posed. "In the mess no one suspects that anything important is going on. A crowd in a public place is best cover possible for people . . . er . . . of our kind." He gave Mallory a glimpse of his dingy bad teeth.

Mallory nodded and said nothing.

Outside a Guards band was marching by, all blaring brass and thumping drums. They were playing one of those old, sad marching tunes of the Old War. Cannon fodder for the front, all young lads and old men, Mallory told himself, heading for Victoria Station and the trains that would take them to their deaths on the other side of the Channel.

If C, ex-Life Guard himself, heard, his grey wrinkled face, steeped in ancient sins and secrets, showed no sign of it. Instead he said in that dry, low voice of his, "We're in a bit of a fix, Mallory."

"Sir?"

"Yanks, you know. They always fuck things up." He tittered at the use of the swear word. It seemed to please him for some reason or other.

"Yanks?"

"Yes. Eisenhower's been on to the PM and the PM's been on to me. Now I'm – er – on to you."

Outside someone cheered the band and the draft. But there was no enthusiasm in the sound really. Everyone, even patriots, it appeared, had lost heart. The war had been going on just too long.

"A flap, sir?" Mallory ventured, eager to know now what C had in store for him.

"Sort of." For a moment C adopted that old, languid Etonian manner that Mallory knew so well. But even that had worn thin over the last terrible years. "Yes," C went on. "The damned Yanks have gorn and lost one of their generals.

Damned nuisance." He finished his sherry while Mallory waited, nerves tingling electrically. Outside the sound of the Guards band had died away.

"Now the PM wants you and your rogues to go and find him." He looked at Mallory as if he were seeing him for the very first time. "Alive," he paused ever so slightly, "or dead . . ."

Three

"Get them knees up . . . Let's have a bit o' movement there, gildy . . . Now then you bunch o' pregnant ducks." The hard voices of the 'staffs', as all the NCOs were called regardless of their real rank, shattered the morning stillness. *"At the double now . . . GET ON PARADE!"*

Smartly the NCOs in their highly polished boots crunched up and down the frozen gravel paths between the Nissen huts of Louvain's military prison, their breath fogging in the air, their cheeks a gleaming, well-shaven red. Cracking their swagger canes against the corrugated iron of the huts' walls, they yelled threateningly, *"Come on now . . . Let's be having yer . . . Last man out's on a fizzer . . . AT THE DOUBLE!"*

Inside the huts the prisoners – deserters, black marketeers, petty thieves and the like – sprang into violent life. It didn't pay to be late on parade here. The staffs were only too eager to take the law into their own hands – four or five of them at a time, all armed with pick handles. Prisoner and guard alike, they had been both brutalised by war and crime.

Up in the commandant's office, the CO and Commander Mallory watched as the prisoners came streaming out of their huts into the frozen snow, swinging their arms to shoulder-height as if their very lives depended upon it. "They come in here as criminals," the Commandant said in his clipped fake Sandhurst accent (he had been an insurance clerk in Holborn before the war), "and we return them as soldiers again." He touched his thin moustache, which looked as if he pencilled it on every morning. "Drill, drill and more drill, Commander. That's our motto inside here. Instant obedience to orders—"

Breaking off, he pointed to a skinny soldier wearing a balmoral and with the lion patch of the 15th Scottish Division on his shoulder. He had slipped and fallen on the slick surface of the parade ground and the RSM was prodding him with his pacing stick, as if he were trying to ascertain whether the fallen soldier were still alive. "Look at that idle man. Deliberately slipping in order to break something. Then into dock for a couple of weeks of lead swinging while his comrades do their bit at the front. Awful type."

The RSM gave the Scot a hefty prod with his brass-shot pointed stick and cried at the top of his voice so that crows in the skeletal trees around the camp rose cawing in hoarse protest, "On yer plates o'meat, you 'orrible little man."

'The 'orrible little man' did as he was commanded and marched swiftly behind the rest. The Commandant smiled thinly and touched his Ronald Coleman moustache as if to assure himself that it was still there. "We don't molly-coddle them inside here, Commander," he commented.

"So I see," Mallory said ironically.

But irony was wasted on the Commandant. He said, "We owe it to the chaps in the firing line. Now that the Huns have started this new show in the Ardennes, Monty needs every man in the line. We're cleaning them out by the platoon – those who will go to fight will have their sentences quashed. We want to get shot of all of them before we move to Antwerp. The powers that be can't have a valuable installation like this overrun by the Boche, can they?" he added earnestly.

"Of course not," Mallory agreed, growing a little impatient. He wanted the Marauders out as soon as possible. All the same he wanted as few people as possible to know that they were something special – not to end their days swiftly as PBI at the front. Belgium was full of spies. The Germans had agents and sympathisers near every Allied camp. After all they had had four years of so-called Occupation to build up their spy-and-sleeper network.

Now the prisoners were lining up on the parade ground, shuffling their feet, giving their uniforms and equipment a last anxious check before the inspection. They tapped their pockets, felt for the brass buttons, pressed their little fingers into the muzzles of their rifles (unloaded naturally) to remove the last speck, tugged at their gaiters, rubbed the toecaps of their boots on the backs of the khaki battle-dress trousers.

Mallory stared hard through the snow which was beginning to fall again in an attempt to spot any of his Marauders. As usual they had got themselves into trouble as soon as he had left them. The day after, they had blown all the Dutch money which had been in the German paymaster's safe, and they had attempted to hold up an Allied paymaster – American – one of those who paid out the troops on a short leave from the front in Brussels. They hadn't reckoned with the toughness of the Yanks, who guarded their pay offices, as if this was back in Chicago in the days of Al Capone. Within minutes apparently, the drunken giggling Marauders had been peering down the barrels of several dangerous-looking shot guns wielded by decidedly unfunny Yanks, military policemen, who obviously hadn't appreciated the humour of the situation.

Mallory sighed and gave up for a moment. They'd turn up. They always did – 'like the proverbial frigging bad penny', as 'Barrow Boy' would have phrased it. He listened to the harsh cries of the staffs, their threats, their crude jokes, their orders. *"Like a bleeding concert violinist . . . get that FRIGGING hair cut . . . Bend down like that again, lovely boy, and I'll be taking the Vaseline to yer tonight, mark my words, laddie . . ."*

Mallory's gloomy thoughts and boredom at the unnecessary delay were interrupted by a polite, even timid knock on the door of the Commandant's office. "Come," the CO cried, all Sandhurst once more.

A bespectacled little lance-corporal, fussy and a little frightened, came in, a sheaf of papers and a clutch of brown official cards in his pale, ink-stained hands. It was obviously the CO's clerk. "Posting orders, sir, and the prisoners' records, sir," he said, puffy, office-worker's face turned to one side, as if he were half expecting a blow across it. "Where shall I put them, sir?"

"Where indeed, man?" the CO snapped. "The posting orders on the desk. The cards to me. At the double, corporal . . . at the double." He half-turned to Mallory and said proudly for his benefit, "Everything's done at the double here – even the staff works like that."

"I see, Captain," Mallory said as below the men were finally brought into line to await the Commandant's normally feared inspection. On this particular morning, however, the military prisoners were more scared of something else: the fact that yet another goodly number of them would be asked if they would 'volunteer' for front-line duty in return for having their sentences 'quashed'. Yesterday the Commandant had dealt with the 'twenty-eighters', men who had received a twenty-eight days sentence. Today it would be the 'fifty-sixers' and prisoners 'on hold', waiting to be court-martialled for sentence. Now Mallory wondered just how he was going to get his Marauders, who were still 'on hold', out without arousing the Commandant's – or anyone else's suspicion. "Do you think we could have a look at your rogues." He gave a mock shiver. "It's beginning to snow hard and I'd like to get back to the wardroom fire as soon as possible." He shivered again dramatically.

The Commandant gave a fake laugh, suggesting he was a hardened veteran, seasoned by months at the front, who had never sat in front of a warm fire in his whole combat career. "All right for some, sir, if you'll forgive the expression, what!"

'Arsehole,' a little voice at the back of Mallory's mind said scornfully. Aloud he said, "Well, we naval types like to look after ourselves, you know. Now to our *moutons*—"

The Commandant looked puzzled at the French word.

Mallory didn't enlighten him. He continued with, "What

I'm after is some hard cases. Men who won't really soldier." He lowered his voice and said significantly, "Useless types who are expendable . . . who won't be any great loss to society if they buy it, if you follow."

"Suicide mission, sir?" Now the Commandant was whispering too.

"Exactly. We still haven't cleared the minefields on the approach to Antwerp." He meant the recently captured great Allied supply port. "Vital to get them dealt with. Can't use Jerry POWs. There'd be a great outcry from those bleeding hearts of the International Red Cross if too many of the German buggers bought it. My Admiral thinks we can use some of your blokes."

"Got you in one, sir," the Commandant said eagerly. "That's why I sorted you out some of our really bad types when you phoned. Thought it'd be something like that. Useless mouths to feed. Be no loss to the British Army if they went for a Burton, what."

"What," Mallory echoed, but again his sarcasm, just like his irony, was wasted on the other man.

The Regimental Sergeant Major, swinging his pace stick back and forth, looking threatening, his drinker's bloodshot eyes fierce, strode along the ranks of the parade, ignoring the snow flakes beginning now to settle on his big, muscular shoulders. "In a moment, you idle men, the officers will come out to read out the names of those of you who have been given the great honour to go up the line." He allowed himself a malicous grin. "We all just know how frigging eager you are to die for frigging King and country. Eh?"

In the second rank, now shrouded in the whirling clouds of new snow, someone broke wind, long, loud and insolent. The NCO whipped round, face red with fury. "What filthy man just farted illegally on parade?" he demanded. "Come on, you filthy man, own up."

As the furious RSM raised his stick and shook it at the prisoners, Mallory grinned carefully. Only a Marauder would have dared to fart on such an occasion. They were there – somewhere in the ever increasing white-out.

Five minutes later, after the Commandant had read out the list of those who had 'volunteered' for the line and they were marching over to their huts to be released to their old units and the certain death that awaited them (for any battalion commander in his right mind would get rid of them first and save his trusted men, who had stuck out the horrors of the front), Mallory was striding along with the Commandant, picking out his Marauders – and a sad sight they looked, too. Bandaged, several of them with black eyes, sticking plaster decorating their bruised faces, they looked as if they had tackled the whole of the *Wehrmacht* instead of a 'bunch o' frigging Yankee nancy-boys' from the US 82nd Airborne who, with the American MPs, had tried to arrest them, as 'Poxy' Peters later described their opponents.

Still, as soon as they spotted Mallory they squared their shoulders like the good soldiers they really were, winked in a couple of cases and even, in the case of Ali Hassan Muhammed Kitchener, attempted a kind of covert salaam.

"I think these are the men I selected, Captain." Mallory halted and frowned, as if he didn't like what he saw through the flying snow.

The Commandant frowned even more. "A bad bunch, Commander," he said, staring at the line of tough, expressionless faces – Peters, Kitchener, 'Lone Star' Jones and 'Barrow Boy' Stevens. "They include a murderer," – he squinted at the men's conduct sheets – "a real spiv, some sort of Hun accused once of high treason," – the CO meant Thaelmann, former member of the German Communist Party and ex-inmate of Dachau Concentration Camp – "and some sort of Gyppo, who reckons he's the grandson of Field Marshal Lord Kitchener."

Mallory nodded, not taking his eyes off his bunch of rogues, every one of them with a tale to tell that would make the genteel reviewers of the *Times Lit Supp* have a heart attack on the spot.

"Crime sheets as long as your arm, Commander," the CO warned him.

"I'll take 'em," Mallory said firmly. The sudden snow storm was just what he needed to smuggle his men out of Louvain's military prison without too many prying eyes seeing them.

"You'll need an escort, Commander?"

"No thank you, Captain. I'll take care of them." Mallory tapped the thirty-eight at his hip. "I promise you they won't escape from me." That one hard blue eye flashed fire and the CO thought it better to say no more. So he contented himself with saying, "The RSM'll see 'em to your transport."

"Thank you."

The CO nodded to the big RSM with the pacing stick, his black shaven jowl covered with talcum powder. "Sir!" he bellowed at the top of his voice so that Mallory standing only a few feet away winced.

"Wheel 'em to the main gate and the waiting fifteen hundredweight." He meant the small truck Mallory had brought with him from Brussels.

"Sir." The RSM swung round in the snow, as if he were back at the pre-war Guards Depot. "All right, you shower, watch it!" Swiftly he rapped out his orders, as the snow beat at his brick-red, black-jowled evil face. "Permission to march off, sir?" he yelled at the CO.

The Commandant touched that pencil-like moustache of his momentarily and Mallory told himself contemptuously that the little prick would savour moments like these to the end of his boring suburban existence. "Permission granted, Sar'nt Major."

"Swing them arms now . . . remember who you is." The little group of Marauders started to march past.

The Commandant braced himself. "Eyes . . . eyes left," the RSM bellowed, bringing his right hand up in an immaculate salute, while Mallory touched his battered cap in a perfunctory manner. As they passed, Stevens broke wind again – loud, long and insolent.

Mallory grinned. No one could get his Marauders down. A moment or two later they had disappeared into the whirling white-out. Mallory's Marauders were going back to war . . .

Four

"*Brrr!*" Like the sound of an irate woodpecker, the American machine gun opened up just as they were about to cross the freezing stream with their wounded and prisoners.

"Down! . . . *Hit the dirt!*" von Dodenburg yelled frantically. He flung himself full length in the snow. A burst of green and red tracer cut the air where his head had just been. Next to him, already crouching, eyes searching for the enemy machine-gunner, Schulze raised his machine pistol. It was like a kids' toy in his big hairy paws. "Yankee barnshitters," he cursed, as next to him, Matz pulled a stick grenade from his boot. The grenade sailed through the air and exploded in a burst of angry, cherry-red flame, flecked with earth and snow, in the same instant that Schulze spotted the dark shapes in the trees opposite and opened fire.

For a minute or two, von Dodenburg let his two old hares fight back, while he surveyed the snowbound terrain and assessed their position. They were in one of the rugged, tight valleys, complete with stream, which ran into the border river, the Our. The Americans were on both flanks. They were obviously waiting for von Dodenburg's party of survivors to cross the stream, hampered as they were by the wounded and prisoners, some of them wounded too, before opening fire when the Germans were trapped mid-stream. Some nervous Ami had jumped the gun and opened fire too soon. Von Dodenburg, his keen, young, arrogant face set and determined, sent up a prayer of thanks heavenwards that the unknown Ami had.

"Sir," Schulze gasped, lowering his Schmeisser momentarily, "it's piss or get off the pot time. There's more of them on the left flank and nine o'clock. See?"

Von Dodenburg did. The Amis, crouched low, were hurrying through the snow-bound firs, dragging a 57mm light cannon behind them. They were about to make sure that von Dodenburg's survivors from SS Assault Regiment Wotan, the most elite unit of the *Waffen SS*, never crossed the *Ihrenbach*. "All right, you big horned ox," he yelled above the angry snap-and-crack of the small arms battle which had now commenced, "this is the drill."

Ten yards away, huddled at the edge of the stream in the frozen mud with the American and German wounded, the latter armed and being used as guards, Horowitz considered, his brain working furiously. The other US prisoners were a sorry bunch – he wondered why the Krauts even bothered with them. They had lost all will to fight. For them escape was out of the question. Naturally, he told himself, he could attempt to take them over and put some backbone in them, force them to follow him. But they'd be a burden, slow him, and in the end probably prevent him from escaping and he knew it was vital that he did so before the Krauts found out his true identity and rank.

He stared at the defenders, now covering the rough-and-ready perimeter. The SS bastards were no amateurs, that he could see. They had reacted correctly to the surprise attack – without orders. But now their leader, the hard-bitten, handsomely arrogant officer with his shaven blond head would have to give orders, make decisions. Horowitz frowned. Which way was he going to attempt to go to get out of the American trap? That was the sixty-four dollar question, as they said these days.

Suddenly, without any apparent reason, the old tale of the mysterious D-Day poles came shooting back into his mind. Before that terrible Tuesday, when the 'All Americans' had dropped into Normandy, those in the know had puzzled over a series of poles that had begun to appear in the pre-invasion aerial photos of the drop zones. In the end they had given up trying to interpret their meaning; there appeared to be no order or system to the arrangement of the poles. On D-Day itself, he and a few others on the staff of the 82nd Airborne had landed next to one of the pole-filled fields. They had eventually found the French farmer who owned the field and had asked him what the poles had been intended for. The Frog had laughed out loud, tugged at the end of his swollen, Calvados-reddened nose and explained that the Germans had ordered all farmers to plant poles in their fields. He had put all his poles in the 'west field' because his 'beasts' didn't like the pasture there and wouldn't eat the grass. So it had seemed to be a good place to get 'rid of the damned poles!'

Now as tracer slugs zipped back and forth in a lethal Morse and an American mortar had joined in the battle, lobbing its bombs with an obscene grunt into the water, he realised that he was faced with a similar situation. There was no use attempting to work out a plan, a system. He would seize the opportunity to escape as it came. The slightest letting down of the Krauts' defences – that had to come soon – and he'd make a break for it, whichever way it took him, away from the stream or over it. After he'd gotten away, he'd work out something else. Famous last words, buddy, he said to himself and then he grasped the branch he was using as a stick to support him in his suddenly sweating palm and prepared to go. Brigadier-General Horowitz, late of the 82nd Airborne Division, was ready.

Von Dodenburg was too, now. He waved to Schulze and cried above the racket and the triumphant cries of the Amis who were getting ever closer. "Take Matz and pretend to attack their left. Keep 'em occupied for five minutes at the most, then take yer hindlegs in yer paws and run."

Schulze cried back, "Will do, sir."

"I'll lead the rest out through there." He indicated the spot higher up where the Amis were setting up their 57mm cannon. "They won't expect me to attack there. *Hals und Beinbruch, Jungs.*"*

"*Hals und Beinbruch, Obersturm,*" Schulze answered

* Literally: 'Break your neck and legs', i.e. happy landings.

and then turning on Matz, he snarled, "Come on, you frigging aspagarus Tarzan. What d'yer want, a frigging written invite?"

Matz snarled back, "Up yours, piss pansy."

"Can't. Got a double-decker bus up there already." And with that piece of scintillating repartee, the two old comrades set off to make their feint.

Von Dodenburg grinned momentarily. Then he dismissed them from his thoughts. Time was running out – fast. He stretched out his right hand, fingers splayed on the top of his camouflaged helmet, the old infantry signal for rally on me; a moment later he was moving purposefully up the height towards the gun. Behind him his teenage grenadiers followed, as if they would do so to the very doors of hell.

Waiting his chance, Horowitz could not but admire the Krauts. SS though they were, they were real soldiers. Even in the elite airborne, you wouldn't get soldiers to follow like that without an argument or explanation. Paras always wanted to frigging well know why. He tested his weight on the stick. Pain shot electrically upwards from his wounded ankle. He fought back the shocked gasp just in time. The wounded teenaged grenadier with the bloody bandage who was acting as a guard was crouched right behind him. Horowitz didn't want to rouse his suspicions.

"*Hoch*," the grenadier ordered. He dug the muzzle of his machine pistol into Horowitz's ribs painfully. Horowitz rose to a crouch. Around him the other American prisoners, a sorry defeated bunch of infantrymen, black gunners and a couple of French attached to the US 1st Army got up too. Obviously, Horowitz told himself, while the officer and the two noncoms played their nasty little games in front in an attempt to stop the attacking 'friendlies', the main body was to retreat down the steep slope and across the River Our far below in the valley, which marked the border with Germany.

Horowitz drew a deep breath. It was going to be now or never. Once they had crossed that river into Germany, he could count his chances of escaping as nil. It was going to be risky, but at least the guards would be diverted. They'd be too busy attempting to keep their balance on the steep, wooded downwards slope and dodging American bullets. The guard dug him in the ribs once more, again painfully. The General stopped himself from cursing the German kid just in time. He didn't want to alert the guard that he was wide awake; he wanted to be thought as dumb and defeated as the rest of the SS's captives. "*Los,*" the kid urged. "*Vorwärts . . . los, Mensch!*"

Numbly, each man wrapped in a cocoon of his own thoughts and fears, they started to stumble down the rocky slope, slipping in and out of the firs, hearing the slugs thwack into the trunks of the trees on both sides, occasionally being showered by a green rain of firs. Horowitz concentrated apparently on keeping his footing and trying to keep up with the rest, as he supported himself, pain-racked on his stick. In reality, however, he was watching the terrain on both sides, looking for a large enough boulder or a patch of firs in which to hide. There wasn't much time left.

Von Dodenburg knew that, too. The Americans with the gun were almost in position. A few minutes more and they'd sink the cannon's trails into the snow-softened earth at the top of the slope and begin lobbing high explosive shells at the men retreating down to the River Our. A flash caught his eye. He knew it for what it was immediately. The scope of a sniper's rifle. He swung round, firing from the hip like some gun-slinger in a cheap Hollywood Western as he did so.

There was a shrill hysterical scream. A flurry of hands in the crown of a tree at 'ten o'clock' to his left. Next instant the sniper came tumbling to the earth to hit it, bounce upwards a single time and then lie there sprawled out in a crimson star of his own blood, set against the brilliant white of the snow.

Von Dodenburg was pleased with himself. That sniper would have been a damn problem if he had not revealed himself so easily. He wouldn't have been able to get any closer to the unsuspecting gun crew. Now they were a matter of a mere hundred metres away and virtually his for the taking.

He surveyed the Amis for a long moment, ignoring the wild battle going on behind him. There were five of them: two at the trails, two at the wheels, all with their rifles slung and concentrating on pushing the ton-weight of the 57mm cannon, and one hanging over the barrel, a tommy gun in his hand. He would be gun-commander. Naturally he'd pick the easiest job for himself, balancing the gun so that the trails at the far end rose.

Von Dodenburg smiled thinly, almost cruelly, to himself. Unfortunately, this time the gun-commander had picked the short straw. He raised his Schmeisser. This time he took careful aim. The body of the unsuspecting American filled his sight, neatly dissected by the crosswires. He took first pressure. His knuckle curved white around the trigger. His breath almost ceased as he controlled his excitement, that old primeval bloodlust which overcomes men in battle. Then he pulled the trigger back with a short, deliberate movement.

The Schmeisser exploded. He felt the jolt in his shoulder. His nostrils were assailed by the acrid stench of burnt cordite. Tracer zipped lethally across the bloody valley. The gun-commander flung up his hands melodramatically. For a moment he poised there, his hands fanning the air wildly, as if he were clawing the rungs of an invisible ladder. To no avail. He screamed one single time, as the unbearable pain hit him. Next instant he slipped from the barrel.

Things happened like lightning. The barrel went up, the trails down. The four men pushing came to an abrupt halt. For a moment they looked completely bewildered as if they couldn't comprehend what was happening. Von Dodenburg didn't give them a chance to find out. "Try this on for collar size!" he cried wildly and spun the muzzle of his machine pistol round. They were in the act of frenziedly unslinging their rifles when the cruel burst hit them. They were bowled off their feet like nine-pins. Arms flailing wildly, they went down, while von Dodenburg kept his finger pressed down hard on the Schmeisser's trigger, pumping lead into their blood-soaked bodies long after they were already dead.

On the other flank Schulze and his undersized, wizened running mate, Matz, heard that crazy, prolonged burst of fire and knew instinctively it was their beloved CO. "Holy strawsack, Schulzi," Matz exclaimed joyfully, "the Old Man's given 'em some stick."

"Hold yer water, currant-crapper, we're not out of it yet." He ripped off a burst at the Amis to his left front and six or seven of them went down, galvanised into violent death throes, all flailing arms and legs, like puppets worked by some crazy puppet-master. Schulze allowed himself a brief smile of satisfaction. "Bet that made 'em cream their skivvies," he commented cruelly.

"Look out!" Matz yelled urgently and ducked.

Schulze did the same. Just in time. The egg grenade exploded just behind them. Red-hot steel slivers hissed through the air everywhere. Schulze yelled angrily and slapped his big paw to his, suddenly bloody, arm. "Frigging lot of iron in this mountain air," he snapped and next instant shot the American who had thrown the grenade, with a bellowed, "That'll learn yer to throw things at yer older and frigging betters."

But the two old hares knew the time for the supposedly tough cracks of cynical, battle-hardened veterans was over. If they didn't move back soon, they'd be dead – very dead – battle-hardened veterans. The Amis had been stalled for a few minutes and they guessed the rest of Wotan's survivors would be well down the slope towards the River Our by now. It was time to go. Matz looked at Schulze. The latter read his mind. He nodded. "All right, old house," – he paused and flung a look to where the CO had just been – he had gone, too, now – "I think we ought to fox-trot back to the river."

"I think I'd rather do the mattress-polka* any day," Matz quipped. "Yes, let's do a bunk tootsweet."

"Tootsweet it is!"

Next moment the two of them were moving backwards to the edge of the slope, stumbling over the dead bodies of the Amis, firing controlled bursts to left and right while the Americans came steadily on, emerging from the woods like hungry timber wolves intent on their prey.

Down below, Brigadier-General Horowitz slung a handful of gravel, shale and snow at his young SS guard, then he was running the best he could into the shelter of the rocks, the slugs whining uselessly off the boulders behind him. And as he ran, his face contorted with almost unbearable pain, still he felt a sensation of elation of a kind he had never felt before. It was as if he had finally flung off all the bonds of convention, repression, duty that had seemed to have constrained him all his adult life. He was alone and free at last.

* SS slang for sexual intercourse.

Five

General James Gavin, commander of the US 82nd Airborne Division, was a worried man. Admittedly the handsome young paratroop commander was as elegant as ever – indeed he didn't look one bit different from the time Mallory had first met him before the Invasion of Sicily in the spring of 1943 just after he had formed his Marauders in the Western Desert. All the same he was worried, Mallory told himself: one didn't need a crystal ball to see that. While outside in the Belgian barracks, which was his HQ, staff officers raced back and forth, teleprinters clacked and telephones rang urgently, the normally cool Gavin drummed on the table with his fingers, as if he could hardly contain his nervous impatience, repeating time and time again, "What a goddam snafu, Commander . . . what a snafu*."

Mallory waited patiently. As he had always maintained, 'even generals wet their knickers'. Not that a fighting soldier like Gavin, whom he admired greatly, did; but he was certainly very agitated, as if it were all too much for him.

Gavin had already told him why, in part. "They dragged us from Sisonne in France in half a daze – we're still recovering from our losses in Holland, Commander. They told us we were going to Werbomont, then Bastogne – both in Belgium. But in the end, understrength, with no transport and heavy weapons to speak off, we landed here in the St Vith and Vielsalm area. I can tell you, Commander, it's been quite a headache." And General Gavin, the most

* US Army slang – 'Situation Normal, All Fucked Up'.

experienced parachutist general in the whole of the Allied army in Europe, had put a slightly shaky hand to his head like a man who was sorely tried.

Now, after a cup of coffee, so strong that Mallory felt it would make his hair curl, at least General Gavin was a little more calm, but not much. It was obvious that he had a lot on his plate. Now, as he had just put it, "Ike," – he meant the Supreme Commander General Eisenhower – "is bugging me from Paris. Just at a time when I'm living from day to day here in Vielsalm. Hell, what am I saying? – *from frigging hour to hour*!" He rose swiftly from his simple wooden chair with the ease of a trained athlete, which he was, and strode over to the big map labelled 'Secret' which adorned the wall. "Look," he announced and ran his hand over the border area, covered with a complicated rash of blue and red symbols. "Here's the St-Vith salient. There's about twenty-odd thousand GIs trapped inside that twenty-five square miles of territory – men from half a dozen units with half a dozen generals in there with them, all giving out conflicting orders."

Mallory smiled sympathetically; he knew what Gavin meant. He had seen some of the survivors. They had appeared at the end of their tether.

"Behind us – here – we've got a trapped SS regiment, plus another couple of SS armoured divisions attempting to free the Krauts trapped up there – at this point, La Gleize," – he tapped the map again – "and at the same time trying to shaft us from the rear end." He forced a smile. "Without the benefit of Vaseline. And it hurts like hell, I can assure."

Mallory returned his smile.

"Now, you're here, with the order from Ike and, I guess, from your Mister Churchill too, telling me I've got to give number one priority to helping you to find and rescue poor old Mo Horowitz, the sorry bastard, after going and getting him captured by the Krauts like that." There was no rancour in his voice at the thought of the extra burden that Mallory was imposing on him, just total, one hundred per cent weariness.

Gavin relaxed a little, his voice quieter now so that the two of them could hear the threatening rumble of the guns from the front. "Mo, that sad sack," he continued, "simply couldn't get used to the idea of being on the staff, you know, Commander. After he was wounded in Holland and couldn't command his battalion anymore, I had him put on my staff – best brain in the whole division he had. But he hated the job, every goddam last minute of it. Any chance he had, he was off in his jeep to visit his old outfit, and if he got lucky, take a few potshots at some Kraut. That's how he got bushwhacked six days ago." Again he sighed.

Outside he could hear Barrow Boy Stevens, known by his comrades as 'Spiv' and sometimes other, cruder names too, saying winningly to some unsuspecting American orderly room clerk, "Now this ain't no ordinary Luger, mate. No sir. This one was carried right throughout the last war by Adolf Hitler personally. I hate to let it go, chum, but . . ."

This time it was Mallory's turn to sigh. His little bunch would rob the Yanks blind if he didn't get them on the road again soon. He'd never met a bunch of servicemen so bent as his Marauders. Hastily he concentrated on the elegant, slim paratroop general once more.

"We know he survived because, afterwards, one of my guys found his helmet." Gavin allowed himself a cynical little grin. "You don't find many helmets belonging to one star generals on a battlefield, I can tell you, Commander. He left it behind deliberately, I'm sure, to tell us that he had been captured."

Mallory nodded his understanding, but said nothing. "Then yesterday, one of our patrols got into a running fire-fight with some SS Krauts trying to cross the River Our back into that goddam Reich of theirs. A corporal who was hit on the western river bank says he saw General Horowitz hobbling down the slope towards the water. The corporal had been hit in the knee so he couldn't go in with the rest of the attack; he just sat there and waited for the medics to come, so he saw Horowitz quite clearly. He's one hundred and ten per cent certain, Commander."

"Yes, I see, General Gavin. So the Hun has still got your missing Brigadier-General, but" – he hesitated but finally he started to pose the question that had been uppermost in his mind ever since C had ordered him to bring back the 'Yank General' 'alive or dead' – "what's so imp—"

"With a name like Horowitz," Gavin interrupted him, "he's a Jew of course. Now he's a Jew in the hands of the SS, goddamit! And you know what that could mean?" Gavin made a clicking movement with his tongue and the thumb and forefinger of his right hand. "They'll have no mercy on him when they look at his dog tag. There's a great big 'H' for Hebrew stamped on it. Sometimes I can't credit the stupidity of our War Department. Do they think we're fighting the frigging war with cream puffs over here?"

Patiently Mallory waited for the overwrought General's little outburst to end before he tried again. Outside, Spiv was saying (while Thaelmann laughed heartily and Kitchener broke in, "You like naughty pictures as well, American boy? High class dirty ones at a modest price . . ."), "Now I can offer yer Hitler's personal pistol at a very favourable price. You see," – there was a sudden professional whine in his voice – "we're going back into the line today and I wouldn't like to think, if anything happened to me, that this priceless heirloom should fall into . . ."

"But it's not because your General Horowitz is a Jew that we've been brought into this," Mallory cut out Spiv's salespitch, "is it, General?"

Gavin looked up at the sudden sharp tone in Mallory's voice and could see why Ike's Chief of Staff had warned him about the 'Limey': 'He knows his job, but remember he's a Class A British bastard, Jim, who doesn't give a fuck about anybody and anything. All he's concerned with is his bunch of hoods and petty crooks – his Marauders, I think Mallory calls 'em. So tread on his toes not, Jim.' Bedell-Smith, the Chief of Staff had added, 'That Limey's one helluva mean son-of-a-bitch!' Now Gavin could see what Ike's fiery chief staff officer had meant.

"No," he said hastily. "But naturally we've got to take that fact into account." Gavin looked around the bare Belgian office with its sole picture, a cheap print of Belgium's disgraced king, now vanished somewhere in Germany. "It's something else." He ended his search of the room, as if satisfied that no one else was listening.

"What?"

"Horowitz is a Bigot!" Gavin said simply.

"You mean like before D-Day?"*

"Yes."

"But what kind of secret does he know?"

"When we drop on the other side of the Rhine, Mallory. In other words, he knows the secret of when our last major offensive starts – the one which will knock Germany out of the war – I hope."

"You mean to say," Mallory exploded, his one eye blazing, "that you let an officer with that kind of knowledge go swanning about at the front? God Almighty, have you Americans got any brains at all?"

"Commander Mallory—" Gavin started.

"Heads ought to roll. Right at the ruddy top," Mallory interrupted Gavin rudely. "While the brass hats play bloody games, the rank-and-file, the poor bloody infantry, get their heads shot off. What kind of bloody war is this?" He paused for breath, his chest heaving angrily, face flushed almost puce.

"Take it easy, Mallory," Gavin tried to appease the irate Englishman, who he knew had seen much of battle, "but war has always been pretty much like that. It always will. Why," he added expansively, "they say Old Boney himself

* 'Bigot' was the code-name given to those who knew when D-Day would take place.

lost the Battle of Waterloo against you Britishers because he ate too rich chow before the battle and had the shits on the day." He smiled winningly.

Mallory gave in. He knew Gavin was a real fighting soldier, who had seen his share of combat in these last eighteen months of war. "Excuse me for blowing my lid. All a bit tense these days, I suppose."

"Of course we are. Now then, back to my unfortunate subordinate, Mo Horowitz, Mallory. Say, what's your first name?"

Mallory returned his smile. "Just call me 'Mallory', General. Everyone does."

"'Kay, Mallory." Gavin rose to his feet and strode back to the big map. He rapped it and said, "Here's the place Horowitz was taken prisoner, probably by stragglers from SS Assault Wotan, which has been stalled some twenty-odd miles into Belgium at a place called La Gleize. Now, Mallory, yesterday our patrol spotted them here coming down from the main road running north-south between Luxembourg City and Belgian St Vith, which is now in Kraut hands, roughly about here, between the village of Hosingen and the border River Our – here. Clear?"

Mallory nodded, damning the fact that he had only one eye. It made seeing small detail difficult.

"Now, we can assume that the SS have taken Horowitz back into Germany between Stolzembourg on the Lux side and probably Gmuend on the Kraut one. That's the way we entered Germany back in September. Christ," – Gavin breathed out hard – "it seems another age now. Who would have thought then, when we believed the frigging war was over, that we'd be in this shitty mess." He shrugged. "No matter, that's the way the cookie crumbles, I guess. 'Kay, so once they are over the Our and back in their own territory, we can safely assume they'll head for one of the *Wehrmacht*'s railheads. Here at Kyllburg, for instance . . . or Bitburg – here to the south. All that terrain is under heavy air attack by our bombers and fighter bombers, so you can figure that they'll be faced with one helluva lot of confusion and will probably travel by night to—"

"General," Mallory interrupted the flow of words firmly, his hand upraised like a traffic policeman halting traffic.

"Yes, Mallory?"

"Do you mean that you want me and my people to penetrate into Germany itself – right in the middle of a battle like this one?" He fixed Gavin's handsome features with that one cold eye of his.

Gavin swallowed. "I know . . . I know," he stuttered somewhat, his composure vanished for an instant, "it's a damned tall order. But it's got to be done . . . whatever the outcome . . ." He let his words trail away into nothing.

Slowly, very slowly, he said, "I understand, General. I know what's at stake. But using the general confusion of the conflict, I am sure we can bluff our way into Germany – I've got a native-born, fluent German speaker in my group. But it means we're going to have to wear Hun uniforms. And you know what that means if we are taken prisoner by the enemy?"

But General Gavim, commander of the 82nd 'All Americans' was not prepared to answer that overwhelming question. Outside Spiv was saying, "Well that's a deal, Yank, then. A case of bourbon, hundred and twenty dollars and a gross of French letters – rubbers to you – 'cos I feel lucky in love." The little cockney crook laughed uproariously. But inside the little Belgian office there was no laughter, no hope or plans for the future. Instead the two officers sat there, as if frozen for eternity like third-rate players at the end of the final act of a fourth-rate melodrama . . .

Six

The *Jabos* – the American dive bombers – came in just before dusk. They came in low, flying down the centre of the valley of the Our. Behind them they dragged their shadows like those of great evil black birds of prey. The hills deadened the sound they made. They were upon the weary party of SS men and their prisoners almost before they knew what had happened. Suddenly, startlingly, the still night air was full of their roar. Angry red flame stitched the lengths of their wings. Red and white tracer sped through the sky like flights of angry hornets. In an instant all was noise, chaos, sudden death.

"Spread out," they cried. "For God's sake – spread out." NCOs urgently shrilled warnings on their whistles. Others booted the slower of the exhausted SS into ditches and behind boulders, crying angrily, "Do you dogs want to live for ever?" Of course, they did. They scattered frantically as the two Lightnings curved in a tight circle, dragging thin smoke behind them, and came in for another attack. This time they weren't going to miss. They lowered their undercarriages. A frantic, angry von Dodenburg knew what that meant. They were going to use the undercarriages as brakes. They'd reduce their speed to near stalling. It would help them to shoot more accurately.

From his hiding place on the slope, hastily pulled down fir fronts covering his hole between two boulders, Horowitz watched the two planes come in, almost hovering above the panicked SS like metal hawks of doom. He wanted them to slaughter the Kraut bastards. All the same the attack could bring disaster for him. If the SS scattered and ran for cover up the slope, as they might well do, they'd make less of a target – and he might be in extreme danger. He was unarmed, in pain and just barely on the fringe of consciousness now. The pain, the loss of blood and lack of food and water these last twenty-four hours were beginning to tell. He had almost blacked out twice already.

Down below like some latterday David facing up to Goliath, von Dodenburg rose from his hiding place. He braced his legs, machine pistol raised, watching the two planes slowly going ever larger in his sight. "Heaven, arse and cloudburst!" Schulze cursed with despair. "Get your head down, sir . . . You haven't got a chance in hell, sir."

Von Dodenburg ignored the fervent appeal. If he could put the Ami bastards off their aim, he might well save his men. The light was going fast in the bottom of the valley. The planes wouldn't have time for another sortie. He tensed. Here they were.

He raised his machine pistol, as the roar of the approaching planes grew ever louder. Now they were racing down the floor of the valley. They twisted and turned expertly. Below, their prop wash raised a white fury of agitated snow. Time and time again it seemed the two US planes might crash into the rock wall. But each time their skilled pilots avoided the crash by a hair's breath. Von Dodenburg watched as the leading plane filled his sights. He hardly dared breathe. He was concentrating his whole being into what had to happen next. He knew he wouldn't get a second chance. His finger curled round the trigger. Behind, crouched low, Schulze waited in an agony of suspense. His whole big body was lathered in a warm sweat despite the freezing temperature. The CO hadn't a chance. Why didn't he drop while he still had time? Next to him Matz was praying. It was probably the first time he had done so since he had been kicked out of his *Volksschule* at the age of twelve for trying to put his hand up his teacher's, *Fraulein* Hartung's, skirt.

Von Dodenburg was totally unaware of his men's concerns. His whole being was concentrated on that lead plane. Despite the failing light he could see its every detail: the dark blur of the pilot's face behind the gleaming canopy; the oil smears around the twin engines; the opening bomb doors . . . He just *had* to knock the thing out of the sky!

"*Jetzt!*" he cried. Next instant he fired. He felt the repeated blows in his right shoulder. Tracer zipped upwards in the lethal Morse. His nostrils were filled with the stench of explosive. Blast whipped his lean, pinched face brutally. For an instant he closed his eyes involuntarily. It was customary. When he opened them again, he could have shouted out loud with joy.

Up above, the leading Lightning had staggered suddenly. It was as if it had run into an invisible wall. For one long moment it seemed as if the enemy plane would hang there for ever. Suddenly, startlingly, things changed. Fire swept the length of the twin rumps like a gigantic, furiously burning blowtorch. The cockpit disappeared in a mass of blinding red. The plane's nose tipped. An instant later it hit the valley floor with a tremendous impact and began skidding across the snowfield, shedding great, gleaming, metallic chunks of shredded aluminium behind it as it raced to its death. Seconds afterwards it exploded in an ear-splitting explosion and fierce blastwave that nearly knocked a bemused von Dodenburg off his feet.

But the SS survivors' ordeal wasn't over. The dead pilot's wingman did something now that caught von Dodenburg and his hard-pressed men completely off guard. He broke off his bombing run, raised his undercarriage and soared high into the darkening sky, as if he'd had enough. But the cheers of the relieved SS troopers died on their lips. He hadn't given up after all. Risking his neck, the pilot came racing down once more, wing machine guns chattering violent fire, spraying the SS with angry bullets. Men went down everywhere, cheers dying in their throats as they did too. In an instant a panic broke out, with the survivors springing over the writhing, contorted bodies of their dying comrades, ignoring their pitiful cries, for the safety of the slope.

In an instant an almost exhausted General Horowitz realised the new danger he was exposed to as frantic, panicked men started clambering among the wooded rocks on all sides. They were heading straight for his hiding place and there was no place he could run to now, that is if he had been capable of running. What was he going to do?

For what seemed an age, General Horowitz was paralysed, apparently unable to move, even to think. The cries of the panicked SS troopers were getting ever closer. Still he couldn't seem to think straight, decide how he still might save himself. Then he realised, as if for the first time, the very great danger he was in. He had dealt with panicked young soldiers before. He knew what they might well do in their unreasoning fear. He had to get rid of everything – anything – that might occasion them to do something crazy.

He hesitated, hand clutched to his neck. His fingers felt and found his dogtags. He had wondered before whether he should throw away the metal discs with their incriminating 'H'. Then he had decided against doing so. He had felt it was a kind of cowardice. But now . . . the threshing and blundering through the firs were getting closer. He could hear the cries of the young troopers as they fought their way out of that valley of death below before it was too late.

Horowitz made his decision. He tugged hard at the metal chain around his neck. It snapped. He hesitated no longer. He flung the chain with its discs as far as he could with the last of his fast-ebbing strength. It sailed into the snow-heavy bushes. He could just hear the faint slither of the disturbed snow and then they were gone. He lay back suddenly absolutely exhausted and waited for that to happen which must.

"Mo," his father had greeted him the first Christmas he had returned to a pre-war New York dressed in his new cadet uniform straight from West Point, "you look great." He had hugged him, visibly moved, while Momma had looked on proudly, tears in her dark eyes. "The Army's filled you out. You've got a fine pair of shoulders on you now, eh." He had beamed at his handsome young soldier son, as if he really meant it.

Then and later, Mo Horowitz had wondered. His father was what was called in the New York theatre crowd a 'play doctor'. That meant he'd been an unsuccessful playwright himself, who had discovered in his failure that he had a talent for rescuing other men's plays. A change of dialogue here, a switch of scenes, a different interpretation of a character and he would turn an off-Broadway production into a Times Square winner. He was even better with Hollywood movie productions. Regularly he'd take the 'Twentieth Century' to Tinseltown, and be paid a tremendous salary for a few days to turn someone else's mediocre product into a movie box-office success.

Naturally, in the '30s, men like his father, educated, liberal, quite wealthy (but not too rich), especially if they were Jewish, did not take kindly to the US Army. New Dealers to the man, who thought the Army was the tool of Republican capitalism, they called the soldiers 'Cossacks', as if they were the representatives of the Czars paid to beat the 'workers' into tame submission to the 'bosses'. His mother who had been born a citizen of Imperial Russia, which she and her family had fled after yet another bloody pogrom, thought pretty much the same.

When he had announced that he had asked the junior senator for New York for an appointment to West Point, they had not objected – they were that kind of liberal. But they had not visited him on the Hudson after his first year at the Point and on that particular Christmas they had asked him in an embarrassed sort of a way not to wear his uniform. Their friends apparently had not taken too kindly to a 'soldier', the bosses' representative, being present at their swank Xmas parties.

Matters had come to a head the day after they had

attended the Academy for his graduation. Obviously they had been proud of him. They had clapped politely after he had received his commission but on the following day, when he had informed them he was being posted to Fort Bliss, his father had said sternly (for him – Liberals, Mo had already learned, could almost never say what they thought straight out; they always had to beat about the bush), "Mo, I think the time has come for you, son, to pack it in."

He had stared at his father in bewilderment and asked why.

"Because, Mo," his father had answered without hesitation, "Jews do not become regular army officers. The people at the top don't like Jews and I can imagine that it's pretty well the same at the rank-and-file level. They think we're not a fighting people and that we're more concerned with living and making money than dying for our country." His father had recently done a doctor job on Bogart and Leslie Howard in the *Petrified Forest*, Horowitz had remembered at that moment, and the Old Man was full of principles and moral choices – turn the other cheek and all that – still, even though it was several weeks since he had returned from Hollywood.

"But there were a lot of Jews at the Academy, Dad," he had protested.

"Token Hebrews," his father had answered with a weary cynical smile and a dismissive wave of his pale weak hand. "The generals are forced by Congress to go through the motions, but it means nothing. Are there any generals of Jewish origin to your knowledge, Mo?"

He had been stymied by the question. For a moment he could not think of any. Besides, his head had been full of that lone black cadet, the only Negro in the whole of the Academy, who had spent the same four years as he totally isolated in his study-bedroom (they hadn't even given him a room mate as was customary). Other cadets had said the 'nigger' hadn't spoken to anyone outside of duty for four long years.

Naturally he had not accorded with his father's wish. It was part youthful stubbornness, part distaste of the circles in which his father moved, part Jewish pride. He'd *make* the Brass aware that Jews were good soldiers, too. But for the first few years of his military career, he had often despaired and felt in the depths of his heart that the 'Old Man' was right after all. He encountered prejudice everywhere. Behind his back he heard the 'red-neck' Southerners, who seemed to make up most of the US Army in those days, call him a 'New York Jewboy' and worse. As for his colleagues, they were mostly older men, time servers for the most part, waiting for pensions, who attributed his energetic efforts to get things moving in the sleepy provincial backwaters where most military camps were located as typical of a 'pushy kike'.

The war had changed everything. Suddenly there were 'temporary officers and gentlemen' drafted into the service by their thousand, a goodly number Jewish college graduates. Now it didn't matter what his ethnic background was. The Army needed bodies, especially West Point trained bodies, who knew the way the Army worked. Within four months he was promoted from 1st Lieutenant to Acting Major.

His standing had changed even more as soon as he had volunteered for the newly formed paratroopers in '41. Big tough hillbilly 'WASPs' flunked out of parachuting training just as often as big city Jewish kids, whose only previous physical training had been raising bottles of Schlitz at the local corner poolhall. Abruptly he was no longer a Jew. He was a man among men. He and they were the elite of the US Army, the men of the future in their jump boots, para-wings, fore-and-aft caps. No one cared a red cent what his or their ethnic origin were.

The jump into France on D-Day (he'd missed Sicily) and then Holland and the Battle for Hell's Highway had done the rest. They were always in the headlines, the 'All Americans' of the 82nd Airborne. They were known throughout the States and abruptly his father was proud of him, very proud. In one of the last letters the Old Man ever wrote to him from Tinseltown, where he was working on another Bogart movie – 'Bogie doesn't just need a doctor, he needs a whole goddam surgical team', he said, 'You were right, Mo, and I was wrong. We need Jews like you, though God only knows what poor Jews we've always been. Thank God you stuck to your guns – I'm proud of you, son.' Three weeks later his father was dead.

Now as Brigadier-General Horowitz lay there, exhausted, drained of all energy, waiting for what was to come, his red-rimmed eyes flooded with tears at the memory of his father's words. Yet at the same time, he felt a fierce pride begin to well up inside him. Come what may, he'd never let his Old Man – his whole race – down. He'd fight the bastards to the bitter end. The sound of big feet pushing their way up the slope was beginning to come ever closer.

Seven

"Did I ever tell yer, Matzi, how I lost me cherry?" Schulze asked lazily. He sat with the ration hip flask, 'flatman', of schnaps in one hand, while he cleaned his foreskin with the bayonet in his other hand. Perhaps it was the latter occupation which reminded the big SS noncom of that event so long before.

"Yes," Matz said, nestling the schnaps issue to his chest like an indulgent mother suckling her firstborn. "But you're gonna tell me agen, I'm sure of that, you big aspagarus Tarzan."

Schulze nodded happily, as he savoured the memory. All around, the weary SS slumped in the thin rays of the winter sun around the camouflaged *Westwall* bunker, occupied by a quartermaster company – hence the schnaps ration. "Kitchen bulls and quartermasters, the thieving bastards, they've allus got some suds and fodder tucked away, sir," Schulze had snorted when von Dodenburg had told them the quartermaster had said he had no spare rations. Schulze had been right. One large right fist the size of the steamshovel had convinced the 'kitchen bulls' they'd been wrong in their assessment of how much 'fodder' they had available.

"I was a bit late at dipping me wick for the first time," he continued. "Almost eleven I think. No wonder if I'm going so impotent so early. The last time I pleasured a piece o' hot gash, I could only do it three times in two hours." He frowned at the dreadful memory.

"Bit worrying when you get to that stage, I shouldn't wonder," Matz said, voice heavy with irony.

But irony was always wasted on his big running mate.

"Yes, it is. Perhaps I ought to go and see the sawbones and get some of them giddi-up pills they give secretly to officers so that they can get their pitiful little peckers up once a month." He paused and took a satisfactory slug of the fiery firewater. For a moment his faded blue eyes lit up and were filled with tears. "Great Crap on the Christmas Tree," he said thickly and wiped his free hand across his wet lips, "that gave me tonsils a surprise. Now what was I—"

"How I lost my cherry and how I was a bit late 'cos I was all of eleven at the time," Matz beat him to it cheekily.

Schulze frowned. "Cocky little bastard, aren't yer," he said withour rancour.

Watching and listening to the two of them, a weary von Dodenburg smiled and withdrew his spoon from the mess tin of 'giddi-up soup', as his stubble-hoppers called the soup made from horseflesh. It was getting cold. Instead he took a sip of the boiling hot canteen of 'nigger-sweat', black and strong and strengthened even more with a shot of the fat quartermaster's own 'personal allowance' of rum. He shuddered at the impact and told himself it was 'just his collar size'.

Inside the bunker, pocked with shell marks like the symptoms of some loathsome skin disease, the signaller was repeating over and over again, "Big six . . . big six . . . over big six . . . do you read me?"

It was obvious that headquarters was not reading the frustrated operator's signal, but von Dodenburg had expected it. Now that the Amis were preparing to counter-attack on the Our – Sauer Line front, they were softening up the German positions with periodic air and artillery bombardments. Naturally the signal wires would be down everywhere.

For a moment von Dodenburg considered, his harshly handsome face set. He had gone to war back in 1939, a young SS officer, filled with fervent patriotism and the belief that the New Germany was about to liberate the decadent old continent of Europe; free it from the dead weight of those perverted old rich men who had run it too long. But over the years the belief in Germany's mission had faded. One by one his illusions about National Socialism had been shattered. Now, after five years of war as a member of the 'Führer's Fire Brigade', SS Assault Regiment Wotan, his trust was reserved solely for his unit. Nothing else mattered – his family, the Homeland, the National Socialist ideals, ultimate German victory. Wotan was now his family, his homeland, his philosophy . . . and Wotan had to be saved. That was his first and really his only priority.

Now as he half listened to the red-faced signaller and watched his young troopers enjoying this time out of war, as they lazed in the weak winter sun, eating their food with the keen appetite of teenage youth, he felt almost like a father to them. He knew that sooner or later the call would come to return to battle for them. But every day he could keep them out of combat would mean a few more lives perhaps saved so that when all this mess was over there would be some of his boys who would help to reshape a defeated Germany in the image of their own tight-knit, loyal community.

Opposite, Schulze had finished cleaning out his foreskin. He wiped the point of his bayonet on his knee and carefully replaced his penis inside his trousers, treating it as if it was a very precious thing, still speaking to Matz all the time. Von Dodenburg shook his head at the action in mock wonder. What terrible rogues his old hares were, but without them he would be lost and the rest of the survivors, too. Schulze and Matz would bully, threaten, cajole, promise twenty-four hours a day just to keep the men going. *But where are we going, Kuno?* a harsh little voice at the back of his mind rasped. Where indeed?

"So the pavement pounder – of course she walked the line – took pity on me," Schulze said. "Whores always do – I've got a likeable sort of a mug, you see."

Matz sniffed, but said nothing.

"She sez, 'Let's see what yer've got inside yer pants, sonny. I'll have a look at it and I'll tell yer if yer'll be able to keep it in me.'"

That was too much for Corporal Matz. "You mean *that* worm?"

Schulze flushed angrily. "What d'ya frigging mean – worm. Why d'yer think I've got this bent shoulders. It's not just from worrying mesen sick about you frigging chocolate soldiers. It's 'cos of the weight I carry beneath my gut. It tugs at my shoulders and that explains why they're bent."

Matz pursed his lips in contempt and made a low, wet farting noise.

Schulze clenched his right fist. "If you wasn't my best friend," he threatened, "I'd polish yer frigging visage for yer."

Matz simpered and said in a fake female falsetto, "Oh Sergeant Schulze, don't be rough with a girl. I might wet mesen." His voice rose to normal and he grunted, "Go and piss in the wind, Schulzi."

His running mate declined the offer and the conversation resumed its normal tone.

Again von Dodenburg sighed in mock wonder and then returned to the problem which agitated his mind at that particular moment. He decided that if the quartermaster and his men could keep out of combat, although they were attached to an infantry division engaged in combat only a couple of kilometres away, he and what was left of his battered command could too. All his lines of communications to his superior headquarters, that of General Dietrich's Sixth SS Panzer Army, were out. He hadn't the faintest idea where the ex-Party bullyboy Sepp Dietrich was at this moment. So, he concluded, he could act under his own orders. So what would an experienced commander, as he was, do under such circumstances?

His first step was obvious. He would get rid of his wounded and in the *Waffen SS* they took particular care of their casualties. They never left their dead on the battlefield for the enemy to collect. Their wounded received the best aid available at the forward field dressing stations and then they were rushed to the nearest hospital.

That then would be his immediate priority: to get the wounded to hospital, wherever that might be, and as the quartermaster would be very unlikely to loan him his horse-drawn transport to do so, he would have to use his own men and the able-bodied POWs to carry the wounded who couldn't walk. Thereafter he would spend more time getting rid of the prisoners to some cage or other.

"Kuno," he told himself, "you are becoming a real slime-shitter, a typical rear-echelon stallion, ready at all costs to avoid having his precious turnip blown off at the front – a feather merchant, first class." He smiled at the thought and wondered what had happened to that SS hero, who had periodically received a new piece of 'tin' from the Führer himself till he had so much he couldn't wear it on his chest anymore, or he would have looked like 'Fat Hermann'.*

He assured himself that that particular hero, named Kuno von Dodenburg, had disappeared in the bloody battle for Stalingrad. Besides Germany, the 'One Thousand Year Reich' that probably wouldn't last into 1945, no longer produced heroes, just bloody-minded fools who were prepared to die for that cheap Nazi slogan of 'Folk, Fatherland and Führer'. No, he, Kuno von Dodenburg, was becoming a new kind of hero – one who wanted to *live* for the future of his Fatherland, not *die* for it.

"Well, the pavement pounder," Schulze was saying, "took a look at it. I could see she was impressed. Her eyes went all funny like and her breath started coming all fast—"

"Why don't yer stick it up yer own arse and give yersen a cheap thrill," Matz suggested in disgust.

Schulze was so carried away by his account of his youthful sexual adventure that he didn't seem to hear the comment. "She sez, 'I do declare, but I think that thing of yours has got real promise. Are you really sure you're only eleven?' I told her I was," Schulze said with undisguised

* 'Fat Hermann' FM Hermann Goering delighted in covering his huge bulk with decorations.

pride. "I knew that because old Rex, you know the corporal in the Second Company who farted a lot till they blew his fart-cannon away, he was a school pal of mine and he said when you was twelve, you got a couple of hairs on it and when—"

"Oh, for frig's sake," Matz cried in exasperation, "piss or get off the pot. Get to the end of it, will yer?"

Von Dodenburg made up his mind. He rose with a little sigh, as if he found it hard to set about his new mission. But he knew it was time to be off. In a couple of hours it would be dark. Before then the Amis on the other side of the line would commence their evening 'hate'. It was their habit: one of a rich, careless nation that didn't have to husband its resources like poor Germany. Their gunners didn't have to ration their shells like those of the *Wehrmacht*. Slowly he walked back to the bunker, gaze falling on the subdued American POWs, those who had survived the aerial attack.

At that moment, he told himself, they didn't particularly look like members of a very rich nation, that legendary continent on the other side of the Atlantic so far away from poor battered, war-torn Europe. They were slumped dejectedly, heads bent, hands on their knees, unshaven faces miserable, all save the one who had attempted to run away. He stared back fearlessly at the arrogant blond SS officer with his rakish cap, adorned with those dreaded symbols, the skull and crossbones of the SS.

Von Dodenburg pulled a face. Of course, the bold American was older than the rest of the POWs. Yet it wasn't that which seemed to make him so defiant. Von Dodenburg couldn't help but think the American had an air of authority about him, that of a man used to giving orders – and having them carried out smartly. But apart from the silver badge of an American paratrooper, he bore no other badges of rank. Even the sleeve of his jacket was bare of sergeant's stripes. He frowned. There was definitely something strange about the Ami. For instance those dogtags which one of the panzer grenadiers had found thrown away into the firs, with the large 'H' for Hebrew stamped on them. Did they belong to the defiant man, and make him a Jew? But if they did, why was the American so determined to hold his gaze? Surely a Jew would be scared shitless at the sight of an SS colonel bearing the legend of the most feared German of them all – Adolf Hitler – on his armband.*

Von Dodenburg shrugged and dismissed the matter. Let the interrogators at the POW Camp worry about that when they'd finally delivered their prisoners to the cage further inland.

Ten minutes later they were on their way again, slogging their way up the hills through burned out abandoned villages, heading for the main road which led to Bitburg where they now knew there was both a proper military hospital and a divisional cage for POWs. Behind them as they left, the silent flashes on the horizon indicated they had just dodged the Amis' evening 'hate' in time.

Before they left, after von Dodenburg had managed to get a couple of horses from a reluctant quartermaster by dint of threats to carry their more serious wounded, he called Corporal Matz over and snapped, "Matz, I want you to keep a special eye on the big Ami over there." He indicated the older POW with the bolder, challenging face. "I know the bugger's wounded, but he's done a bunk once already. I don't want him trying it on again. You never know what he knows. Keep your glassy orbits *peeled*, please, Matz."

"Like the proverbial tinned tomato, sir," Matz had promised. "Anything to get away from Schulze . . . I've had a noseful of his shitting stories."

Now, each man wrapped up in his own thoughts, concentrating on the steepness of the climb, they plodded on into the ever-growing darkness in the east. Now the rays of the weak winter sun had disappeared, the SS troopers in their battle-stained threadbare uniforms started to feel the cold.

* Wotan belonged to the premier SS division – 'The Adolf Hitler Bodyguard'.

Here and there they shivered audibly. But whether they did so from the cold only, von Dodenburg was not prepared to guess. Instead he forced his mind firmly to stay on the task at hand. Five minutes later they had disappeared into the night. Behind them they left the wind whistling through the firs. Above, a spectral moon started to shed its silver, ghostly rays on that war-torn hill. The world this December night had seemingly gone to sleep – or had it . . . ?

PART TWO

Enter Mallory's Marauders

One

The Plaisir d'Amour was packed with officers of half a dozen Allied armies. Most of them were drunk. All were clad in an amazing variety of winter uniforms. There were peroxided French whores everywhere, painted ladies with sweet smiles and calculating eyes like cash registers. They were pouring the high priced sugar water, masquerading as champagne, down their throats, as if they really enjoyed it, making scratches on the beer mats for each bottle they downed for the 'reckoning' which would come later. Business was booming.

The air was blue with smoke. The noise was tremendous. Deep masculine voices chortled and shouted in half a dozen languages. Drunken women screeched and giggled hysterically. They wouldn't be spending the rest of the night in their own beds, Lt Hilary Kluth, known behind her back at Supreme HQ as 'Casualty Cunt', told herself. Indeed, she thought, as the waitress dressed as a man complete with painted-on moustache and too large monkey suit, brought her her double scotch, most of the women looked as if they had not spent the night in their own beds for a very long time. She sighed and coughed in a masculine way and took a stiff drink of her black market scotch. In Paris this December the stuff was worth its weight in gold.

Lt Kluth of the American WAC didn't particularly like the Plaisir d'Amour. She hated the drunken officers, brutalised by the front, intent on indulging in their swinish pleasures – drink and cheap women – before they were sent back to the line to have their heads blown off – hopefully. All the same it was the only place in Paris that she knew where she could find solace in a woman's arms and – God willing – sometimes indulge herself too. There were other lesbian circles in Paris: she was vaguely aware of them. But they were meant for Parisian society women, intellectuals, aristocrats, writers and the like. They were not for the likes of Hilary Kluth, a middle-aged ex-grade school teacher with the suspicion of a moustache, who spoke hardly a word of French and who spent most of her nights alone in the BOQ (Bachelor Officers Quarters) reading the *Stars and Stripes* and drinking herself to sleep.

It had been that great overwhelming loneliness, the ache, the longing that sometimes swept through her body and reduced her to tears that had first started her on what she called to herself 'the downward path'. She needed money to indulge herself and it was the only way she could obtain sufficient in order to pay for those special one night stands which kept her going until the unbearable longing overcame her again.

In two days it would be Christmas and she suspected she'd be working then, too. All day the casualty reports had been coming in from the front. Her boss, that swine Major Faust, with her big paws everywhere, had calculated the US Army had already lost 20,000 men in the first week of the German surprise attack. And there was no let-up in sight. The casualty lists would keep pouring in. So this night she would enjoy herself, come what may. He had promised her money and one could say one thing about the Krauts – they'd pay dead on time. She looked at the young harassed waitress acting as a man, who was doing her best to free herself from a drunken Canuck at the next table and thought, with a sudden weakening of her fat, dimpled knees, she's worth a sin or two. Dare she ask her next time she came with the scotch? She swallowed hard. God, how many times had she been rebuffed in the past! Now in a foreign land where no one knew or cared about her and with plenty of greenbacks in her pocket, she wasn't rebuffed so often. Would she say—

The unspoken question came to an end abruptly. A roll

on the drums. A slim, but middle-aged woman dressed as a man sprang onto the tiny stage, with consciously youthful energy. There was a drunken cheer from the men. They knew what was coming. "Come on, lady," the drunken Canadian officer yelled, "Get on with the frigging dirty bit!" There were roars of agreement.

"Ladies and gentlemen," the Frenchwoman began in fluent American-English.

"What bloody ladies?" someone cried. He was answered by a roar of drunken laughter.

The woman ignored the interruption. She was used to them. "Tonight I give you a spectacle, unlike any in Pig Alley." She used the GI term for Place Pigalle. "I give you—"

There was a weary roll on the kettle drums of the little Bal Musette band behind the stage.

"—Sue and Suzette!"

Suddenly, startlingly, the light went out. The drunken Canuck cried, "Take yer frigging paw off'n me knee, Charley. I'm a frigging virgin."

The audience roared with laughter. Lt Kluth frowned and cursed. She couldn't see the young waitress for another scotch and the other.

A spotlight flashed. The place was transformed. It was no longer tawdry, cheap. It was filled with a silver, Christmassy light. Kluth was moved. It reminded her of Christmas back home as a kid before life had started and she had been happy. Behind, someone moved the thick felt blackout curtain which covered the entrance to the cellar bar. She felt a sudden chill of icy night air. But it was over in a flash. Besides she was concentrating on the tiny stage now. The rest were too. A kind of tense expectation that something very different, unusual, was about to happen filled the crowded room.

Kluth licked her thick red lips which were suddenly very dry. The spot had moved to illuminate two women at the rear of the little stage. Both were motionless – they could have been statues – or dead. Both were completely naked, too. Kluth could see the goose-bumps on their powdered bodies.

The older of the two, her face stamped with a hawk-like, upper-class look of absolute dissipation, sat bolt upright in a hard chair. In front of her crouched the younger one in the position of supplication, hands upraised, her breasts hardly perceptible, the nipples tinted a deep red. She had no pubic hair, in contrast to that of the older one, which was thick and bushy and obviously dyed its raven black colour. Kluth felt herself overcome by a kind of weakness, almost as if she might faint, though her heart under the khaki WAC shirt thumped away crazily.

A drum began to beat. It was almost like the steady throb of a human pulse. Slowly the younger woman seemed to awake, come to life. She reached out a delicate child's hand. She released the golden band which held the older woman's hair. It cascaded down. The young woman rose. Standing so close with her slim stomach that she seemed to be inviting the older woman to kiss her naked breasts, she started to stroke her hair. The thump of the drum increased. Lt Kluth felt herself beginning to sweat. God, wasn't it exciting! How she longed for that young nude woman to do something like that for her. It was more than just sex – it was love!

There was the slight scrape of a chair near to her. She frowned angrily. She hoped she wasn't going to be disturbed by some drunk. She wasn't. A hoarse voice whispered carefully, "It's me – Pepe. Don't turn round. Don't move. Watch the girls. In a minute . . ." It was her contact. She cursed. Why now? Just as she was really beginning to enjoy herself. ". . . I move."

The tempo of the drumbeat was increasing now. On the stage the older woman had slumped in her chair. She thrust her large breasts forward voluptuously. It was as if she could hardly bear the tension. Her mouth drooped. She had opened her naked legs. A sheen of sweat had broken out over body. She could have been covered in a film of Vaseline.

"You like it, *hein*?" the contact whispered. There was a

malicious knowing note to his words. She ignored them. She was too entranced by what was happening on the stage. Already she could feel herself beginning to get wet between her sturdy, unshapely legs. She bit back a groan of pleasure just in time.

The young girl ceased stroking the older woman's hair. The latter mouthed unintelligible sounds. They might have been obscenities – or cries of endearment.

Suddenly, almost startlingly, the girl bent and touched her lips to the great dark-brown right nipple of the other woman. She shuddered. The audience did, too. The older woman sucked in her stomach muscles as if in anticipation. The drumbeat grew ever quicker and louder. Now it was like a pulse racing at fever-pitch.

Quietly her contact said. "Count to three . . . I shall watch . . . When I say 'yes', please give me the list under the table . . . Your money is in the envelope near your glass . . . It is correct."

Now she didn't care about the money, the secret list – anything. Her whole being was concentrated on what was happening on the stage. Still she forced herself to count underneath her breath. "*One* . . ."

On the stage a gramophone record had taken over from the drum. Its music was blatant now in its sexuality. The older woman's hips began to grind in time to the music. The younger woman sucked and sucked at her breast. The older woman jerked her head back and forth, as if she were being choked. Her mouth was loose, slack and wet. She dribbled liquid. Once her fingers, formed into rapacious claws, sought to seize the other woman's petite breasts. She checked herself in time. She let them fall a little helplessly.

"*Two*!"

The older woman's legs were wide open now. It was as if she had totally forgotten the audience. She was moving her loins back and forth. Her teeth were bared fiercely. The music was becoming ever more frenzied. "*Fuck*," she was gasping, "*fuck . . . oh, do fuck . . .*" The spectators were sitting on the edge of their seats. Even the drunken whores had fallen into a rapt silence.

"*Three.*"

A hand touched the WAC officer's knee. She jumped. It was Pepe. Not taking her eyes off that tremendous spectacle on the little stage, she removed today's list of casualties from her slingbag and pushed it towards the unseen contact sitting just behind her.

"*Bon*," he whispered and then added with a sneering tone, "*Alors, sale con, tu est—*"

"Sock it to her, babe!" the drunken Canadian couldn't stand the tension any more. He staggered to his feet dangerously and began to weave his way towards the stage, grabbing with frantic fingers at the brass buttons of his flies. "Let me get there . . . I'll give her a taste of some good old Maple Leaf dick, guys . . . Make way—" The words died on his lips as a harsh military voice commanded, "Freeze it . . . Everyone freeze . . . and no funny business or there'll be trouble!"

"What the hell?" someone cried. A pistol shot rang out. Lt Kluth felt the casualty list whipped from underneath her fingers. On the stage the older woman screamed. The younger one flew at her and threw her arms round her neck protectively. As the main lights went on, Lt Kluth could see just how aged and raddled the older one's neck was.

Suddenly MPs, white helmeted and swinging their white clubs purposefully, were everywhere. For the first time Lt Kluth realised just how much danger she was in. She rose. A heavy hand dropped on her shoulder. Curtly, an official voice snapped, "Hold it there, sister." She looked up in alarm. A big MP sergeant was staring down at her.

"What's going on?" she quavered.

He shrugged. "You'll find out soon enough, sister." He didn't even attempt to use her rank and because he didn't, she knew she was lost. At Supreme Headquarters at Versailles they had found out about 'Casualty Cunt' at last. She hung her head. Unfeeling, the waitress in the male 'money suit' pushed by the grinning MP Sergeant and thrust a scrap of paper in front of the female officer. "*L'addition,*" she demanded threateningly, pretty face grim. She'd already learned to recognise a victim. The fat American cow was one.

Numbly Lt Kluth pushed the envelope with the money towards the girl. "*Ca va?*" she asked without looking up.

"*Ca va,*" the waitress agreed and didn't even bother to count it. The Sergeant's grin grew even broader. "That's the way the cookie crumbles, sister," he said. "Up one day, down the next." He reached out his big paw and she was too broken even to try to avoid it. "'Kay, let's go. The paddy wagon's arrived."

Tamely she let herself be led out into the freezing night air outside. French *flics* and American 'snowdrops' were everywhere. It was a big operation. Vaguely Lt Kluth wondered what all the fuss was about. After all, she simply passed over the details of the poor stiffs who had gotten themselves shot or were missing. What was so important? Her train of thought came to a sudden end. In the blue beam of one of the police halftracks, she saw him. The contact she knew only as Pepe. The little runt was sprawled dead in the dirty slush of the gutter. In his hand he held the list she had just given him. Silently, her shoulders heaving as if she were suddenly broken-hearted, she began to sob.

Two

The young Counter Intelligence Corps (CIC) officer caught up with Mallory and his Marauders as they were planning their breakout from the encircled Belgian town of Bastogne. All day long the German grenadiers of the 26th People's Grenadier Division had been probing the defences of the place, trying to find a weak spot in the paratroopers' line. But they had failed to do so; now the barrage had faded away to a low menacing rumble, like that of some sulky primeval monster cheated of its prey. Everywhere, both defender and attacker had gone to ground, trying to find cover to escape the freezing arctic temperatures of the night.

Hurriedly the young American officer was ushered into the icy room they had been given in the paratroopers' HQ located in the town's Belgian barracks. He looked beat, his overshoes heavy with snow and mud, a loose pistol stuck in his belt. But he was still keen and so eager to pass on his news from Paris that he took only a few sips from the scalding black coffee that Kitchener had brought in.

"Commander," he said hastily, "the Krauts know."

"Know what?" Mallory asked gently. The young officer had a nightmarish journey behind him, including slipping through the German lines to the south; he was going to give him a hard time.

"About the General."

Mallory whistled softly and said, "Tell us more." Around him, his men's faces, hollowed out to death masks in the weak light of the single naked electric bulb, craned forward to catch the newcomer's words.

Hastily the Counter-Intelligence man told them of the treachery of Lt Kluth and how she had been passing over the daily casualty report prepared personally for the Supreme Commander to the enemy for money. "Yes, I understand," Mallory said patiently when the American was finished and he indicated that the young officer should take another sip of his black coffee – 'java', the American called it for some reason or other. "But why should that endanger our mission?"

There was a mumble of agreement from the others and Peters, the earnest young ex-Guardsman who had won both the DSM and MM for bravery, but had been sentenced to prison for five years due to a momentary act of cowardice, said, "I've never heard of casualty lists being exactly serious, sir." He snapped to attention as he remembered he was speaking to an officer, even if he was only an American one.*

The American said, "Oh, they're very useful in the right hands. They give the Krauts the kind of extra little details they can use in their propaganda campaigns for example. That Lord Haw-Haw of yours—"

"Not mine," Spiv commenced hotly, but Mallory silenced him with a fierce glance from that one eye of his.

"When Haw-Haw broadcasts to the UK, he can usually beat your War Office with the details of so-and-so being safe and well. That pleases some mother or other and makes her and her neighbours think the Krauts are both kind and infallible."

"Hardly of world-shaking importance," Mallory commented softly.

* Peters, Albert, b. 1920. Education: Durham Street Council School, Newcastle. Joined Coldstream Guards 1938. Service: Palestine 1938; France 1940; posted to Western Desert 1941. Awarded DSM and MM 1942. Arrested for cowardice under fire in Italy 1943. Sentenced to five years' hard labour. Joined Mallory's 'Marauders' that year.

"No. Sometimes, however, they use this info for military purposes as well, Commander. Last week, for example, the Krauts fired a V-1 at Oldham near your Manchester. It was packed with the latest info on new prisoners of war from that area. Anyone who picked up a leaflet with the info was asked to pass it on to the relatives concerned and—"

"Yes?" Mallory asked, puzzled.

"Then drop a line – the relatives I mean – to the POW back in Germany. It was a beautiful scheme, but your people caught on to it just in time and stopped anyone writing. You see," he added swiftly when he saw that Mallory still hadn't got it, "the replies would have given away to the Krauts where the flying bombs had fallen. They are notoriously difficult to bring on to a target. The info from Oldham which their planners needed for targeting would be obtained from the street addresses of those who replied."

"Cunning bugger, yer old Jerry," Spiv said. "I swear some of 'em must have growed up in Petticoat Lane. What do you think, Thaelmann?"

Thaelmann, his hard-bitten tough face, which looked as if it had been carved out of a slab of granite, revealing nothing, grunted, "Petticoat Lane – what is that?" He spat drily on the floor of the room and added "You English, you just never take things seriously."*

The young CIC officer frowned at the obvious Kraut accent, but kept silent. Instead he waited until Mallory spoke again to ask, "All right then, what exactly does the Hun know about our target?"

* Thaelmann, Ernst, b. 1910. German. Education: Max Planck Gymnasium, Hamburg. Full-time official, KPD (German Communist Party). Arrested and sent to Neuengamme Concentration Camp 1933. Escaped 1934. Went underground. Fought in Spanish Civil War. Joined French Foreign Legion 1939. Arrested Dover, suspected of high treason 1940. Joined Mallory's 'Marauders' 1943.

The young CIC officer frowned suddenly, as if he had abruptly remembered something unpleasant. "This: that we have lost a brigadier-general of the 82nd Airborne Division, named Horowitz. That he was captured by a standing patrol of German SS. We assume that they belonged to the survivors of the SS Regiment Wotan, trapped and nearly wiped out at a place up the road from here called La Gleize."

Mallory nodded his understanding and waited for the young American to continue. "We are naturally very vague about what happened then. Unless General Horowitz was wounded and was unable to do so, we can assume he got rid of his badges of rank and anything that would identify him as a general. It's airborne standard operating procedure. In the paratroopers, generals fight at the side of privates."

Spiv made a movement with his right arm as if pulling a lavatory chain and said cockily, "Pull the other leg, mate, it's got bells on it."

"Shut up, Spiv," Mallory snapped.

"Sorry sir," Spiv said, and under his breath added for the benefit of the other Marauders, "for frigging well living."

"All right, so what could the list that the Hun bought from your traitor woman tell 'em that would bring you here post-haste from your nice cushy billet in Paris!"

The officer actually blushed. "It *is* in the line of duty, sir . . . Well, the casualty list not only specifies the usual things – rank and the like – but also it notes the casualty's place of enlistment and his religion." He hesitated. "Both bad news I'm afraid for General Horowitz."

Far off, dampened by the howl of the night wind coming straight in across that snowy plain outside, Mallory could hear the faint rattle of tracks; and he didn't need a crystal ball to know they could only be that of enemy armour. The Huns were going to attack Bastogne's perimeter yet again. It was time that they got out of the beleaguered German town.

"The General entered the service at Forest Hills, in Queens, New York – a mainly Jewish district, sir," the

CIC officer continued, "and his religion is Hebrew. The Krauts only need to have him stripped and they'll see—"

"He's had his dick docked by the Chief Rabbi," Spiv broke in cheerfully.

"Yes," the American answered unhappily. "They'll put two and two together and come up with the fact that they've got the Jewish General Horowitz of the 82nd Airborne in their hands and . . ." His voice trailed away to nothing, as if he dare not think that particular unpleasant possibility to its logical end.

"They'll work on him," Mallory did it for him, his voice grim.

"In Gestapo they boast they can even make a mummy talk," Thaelmann said in that harsh North German voice of his, his gaze far away as if he were thinking of the tortures he had undergone himself before he had made his daring escape from Neuengamme.

"And once someone starts to squeal," the CIC officer said, "it's my experience they never stop. It's some sort of compulsion. Get it off your chest, the whole shebang and hope to have peace at the end of it."

"Yes," Mallory agreed, "and then they'll find out his Bigot classification and everything that goes with it. Christ, what a mess." He pulled himself together. All right, so what can you tell us about where General Horowitz might be now. If we're going to try to get him back before he starts to sing, we must have some idea of where the SS will be taking him – a central holding cage, something like that."

The CIC officer said, "You've got a picture of the border area around here in your head, Commander?"

Mallory indicated he had.

"Well, we figure the Krauts will be taking him out of the Eifel to one of the railheads – Kyllbury, Phillipsheim, Bitburg or the like."

"That's pretty damned vague, Lieutenant."

"Yes, I agree, but we don't think it's there they'll keep

him. There are POW cages in all those places, but they are *Durchgangslager*. You know the word?"

"Yes, transit camps."

"Exactly."

Outside, whistles were shrilling and harsh impatient voices were crying, "OK, you guys . . . haul ass . . . Stand to your weapons . . . HAUL AA-SS!" Somewhere close by, a machine gun started to rattle. The Germans were getting closer.

"But there's a large-scale transit camp just on the opposite side of the River Moselle not far from the city's main station—"

"Yes, go on," Mallory urged. Time was running out, he knew that.

"We think from serial recon and interrogation of Kraut prisoners that they collect their POWs there and then ship them out from Trier station up to Koblenz where there's a railway bridge intact over the Rhine – it's too well protected by flak for our flyboys to knock it out – though they've tried often enough."

Hastily Mallory absorbed the information. "So you think we've got to stop Horowitz and his escort before they get to Trier, Lieutenant?" he said.

"Yes, once they ship him out of Trier we've lost him for good. Most of the Kraut POW camps, the permanent ones, are to the east of the River Elbe crossing right over Eastern Germany into Poland. It's to make it more difficult for our guys to escape." He paused and looked down at his black felt overshoes in a downcast, hangdog fashion before adding, "It's rescue him before Trier, or the Chiefs of Staff in Washington will have to change their whole plan for the rest of the war, Commander."

On any other occasion, the fiercely patriotic Commander Mallory would have corrected the young American with: 'and the British Chiefs of Staff as well'. But not now. The situation was too grave to worry about niceties. Instead he said, "Any suggestions, Lieutenant?"

"Well, sir," the American answered, "As you already know, the situation at the front here in the Ardennes – Eifel is very fluid. But it has one advantage – for us."

"What, pray?"

"The Krauts have virtually emptied the rear areas of troops. Our aerial recon has shown that." The young American officer waited till a burst of heavy machine gun fire had ended before continuing with, "Once you're through the enemy's main line I think you should be in the clear, Commander."

"Famous last words," Spiv said in a funeral voice.

"Shut up," Commander Mallory snapped routinely. Already his mind was racing electrically at the information he had just received. Of course the American was right: once a front had settled down with patrols, sentries, guards and the like in place, carrying out a regulated daily routine, it was always damnably difficult to get through. The time to do that was when everything was in a state of flux, with the fighting men in the line too busy looking after their own hides to worry about things happening beyond their ken. "You're right," he said, his mind made up. He looked around in the same instant that the American brought out the leather sack from inside his Ike jacket. "Are you prepared to have a bash at it, lads?" he asked quietly. He knew naturally that he could order his Marauders to carry out the dangerous mission ahead – he could even threaten them with a return to the feared 'glasshouse'. But the Marauders didn't function like that: they were as democratic as a military unit could be; they made their decisions on the basis of a majority. One by one they nodded their heads or indicated by a shrug of the shoulders that they didn't mind one way or the other. Kitchener* even gave one of those

* Kitchener, Ali Hassan Muhammed. Volunteered for British Army 1939, claiming he was a descendent of the *Sirhar*, Lord Kitchener. Wounded twice. Court-martialled for looting. Sentenced to five years' imprisonment. First recruit to the 'Marauders' 1942.

gleaming smiles of his, saying, "There will be a reward, sir, perhaps?"

It was as if the American authorities back in Paris had known that Kitchener would have made such a request in advance. For as the young CIC officer untied the strings of the leather bag, the Marauders caught a glimpse of gold.

Kitchener's eyes sparkled. "The blessed Horsemen of St George," he cried and slapped his skinny, brown hands together in an expression of sheer delight.

"Horsemen of St George?" the CIC officer echoed in bewilderment.

"Yes, sovereigns," Mallory enlightened the puzzled officer. "Widely used throughout the Middle East by us as bribes."

The young officer grinned for the first time since he had reached besieged Bastogne. "That's exactly what these coins are for. The Krauts are a corrupt people. In an emergency, you might find they come in useful. You'll have to sign for them, of course, Commander."

"Of course," Mallory agreed with heavy irony.

Ten minutes later, while the young officer relaxed with yet more of his scalding hot 'java', they were on their way, groping their way along the narrow second-class country road that led out of Bastogne and on the way to German-held Niederweiswampach and the German border beyond. On all sides the battle was flaring up now. Green and red flares shot into the dark sky. Guns flashed. Tracer zipped back and forth lethally. Behind Mallory in the lead, an American grease gun slung over his arm, Spiv breathed, "Oh, what did Mrs Stevens' handsome son ever do to get into this pail o' shit?"

But there was no answer forthcoming to that overwhelming question. They plodded on.

Three

It was unearthly cold. The icy wind raced across that snow-bound Belgian plain at fifty miles an hour. It lashed their faces with razor-sharp particles of snow. Their eyelashes and brows were white with hoar-frost; they looked like very old men, hunched against the wind. Every fresh breath was as if a sharp blade had been plunged into their lungs. Infinitely slowly, they slid and stumbled across that unrelenting, never-ending blinding waste, each new step demanding a tremendous effort of will.

Only habit, training and an iron discipline kept them going – and that flickering, ever-present desire to stay alive in a world that was latently hostile and threatening. For even Spiv, that born eternal optimist, had no illusion about what would happen to them if they were captured. What German (or for that matter American) soldier in his right mind would hesitate? They'd be lined up against the nearest trees and shot out of hand. Who would be bothered with prisoners when it was hard enough to keep oneself alive?

In the lead, Mallory, as hard pressed as the rest of the Marauders, tried to keep to his chosen compass course the best he could in that bitter winter landscape, where there were no landmarks. Even the most recent ones, wrecked tanks, shattered cannon and trucks, dead bodies, were already disappearing rapidly beneath the snow flurries which fell at regular intervals. It was as if they were the last men alive on the face of this earth, as they crawled bent almost double across that winter landscape.

But Mallory, as numb and deadened as his brain was

by the fury of the elements, knew that wasn't so. Now and again the grey, sullen gloom lifted to reveal the ugly red flashes of light and the puffballs of grey smoke which indicated an artillery duel. Once they saw a squad of Shermans scurrying for the safety of the rear, leaving behind them the smouldering burning wrecks of their fellows, until the elements closed in once more and it was as if they hadn't been there in the first place. Oh yes, he told himself more than once, the enemy was out there everywhere. One wrong move and they'd encounter them and then . . . Mallory didn't dare that particular thought to an end.

About two that afternoon, Peters's nostrils began to twitch. His long, red nose wrinkled more than once. He turned his neck to left and right slowly, as if it was worked by rusty steel springs. Peters, the product of the hungry '30s in the North-East, had smelled cooking and Peters's 'educated hooter', as Spiv called it, never made a mistake when it came to food. Someone close by was cooking a meal. Peters sniffed again to make sure. There it was – the odour of cooking meat. A slow stream of liquid started to trickle down his unshaven chin. Anticipation! Peters was (to use Spiv's evocative phrase of 1944) losing 'joy juice'!

Spiv noticed immediately. He looked interested. His frozen face broke into a wary smile. "Am I right, old mucker?"

Peters nodded, nostrils still twitching.

Spiv licked his frost-cracked lips. "Peters smells grub, sir,"

Mallory stopped and wiped a few snowflakes from his dripping, brick-red face. "Sure? . . . Where?" he asked laconically. He simply hadn't the strength to exert himself more.

Peters pointed, equally slowly, as if it took a great effort for him to raise his arm. "Over there, sir".

Mallory narrowed his eyes to slits against the driving wind. He could just make out a thin stream of smoke a quarter of a mile or so away. It wavered, shimmied and disappeared again into the white-out. But it was there all right. Over there someone was living, keeping warm, cooking.

Mallory made up his mind. He had to get his men out of the cold for the night. They had already passed through the thin crust of German front-line troops. If they were Jerries over there, they'd be service personnel, old-aged behind-the-desk warriors. They shouldn't be too difficult for his hairy-arsed Marauders to tackle, even if there were so few of them. "All right, chaps," he decided. "We'll have a look-see. Take it easy though, we don't want trouble if we can avoid it. Thaelmann."

"Sir," the German communist snapped, as if he were in the Brigade of Guards. Communist, he might be, Mallory told himself, but he was one hell of a disciplinarian.

"You shadow me. The rest of you spread out and follow."

They nodded their understanding. There was that old significant sound of slipping off safety catches and jerking back bolts, which had always seemed to Mallory to have a jarring note of finality about it, and then they were moving forward through the white gloom to the lonely house . . .

"*Carbonnade*, the Belgies call it," Peters explained as he dipped the ladle in the great cauldron, inhaling the delightful smell that came from it, and gave the rich mixture another stir. "Bits of beef and pork, boiled in beer to make a kind of stew . . . the kind yer mother makes." He beamed happily, his face suddenly red as the hot steam wreathed about his frozen features.

"My mother could burn water," Spiv said cynically, looking around the low kitchen, dominated by the great long oven, white tiled, with little drawers everywhere.

Peters, the ex-Guardsman, ignored the remark. He was concentrating on the stew bubbling away merrily in the great pot. He said, "Peasants make it. Lasts them for days. They keep re-heating it like this while they're out at work doing whatever peasants do."

"Peasants – my arse!" Spiv sneered. "What frigging peasants can afford beef and pig and what frigging peasant in his right mind would be out in frigging weather like this? Come off it, mate. Get yer finger out."

Stevens didn't seem to hear. Carefully he dipped the ladle in the rich mixture and with a look of bliss on his face blew on the steaming mixture before he ate it. At the door, still wary, Thaelmann said, "Don't eat it all, you greedy pig. Think of your comrades, man."

Mallory let the usual chat go back and forth past him, not really taking it in any more, as he considered their position. They had scouted the outside of the tumbledown farmhouse carefully. There had been no sign of tracks, human or mechanical, anywhere. But that was understandable. With the snow coming down now in a solid sheet, as if it would never cease again, all tracks would be obliterated in a matter of minutes. All the same the cockney ex-barrow boy Spiv was right. Peasants wouldn't be cooking a meal of that sort in the middle of battle this December, when meat cost a fortune on the black market. Even if it was their own meat, they'd sell it at some extravagant price rather than scoff it themselves. Besides they certainly wouldn't leave it on the stove for any Tom, Dick and Harry to come and nobble it, just like that. No, there was more to it than that.

He spoke. "All right, lads. Every man helps himself to a mess tin of the stew. But he keeps his weapon at his side while he eats it and then we do a proper search of the outbuildings. I don't want us to be caught with our knickers down now when we're about through the Hun lines."

Spiv said brightly, "Shall I pass out the napkins and the fingerbowls, sir?"

Mallory smiled. The cockney, true to his native breed, was a great breaker of tension. The others weren't impressed. They, like Mallory, must have suddenly felt that the warm, cheery atmosphere of that country kitchen, with the merry red flames of the oven reflected on the white-plastered walls, had changed; become strange and somehow threatening. They ate the rich stew in tense silence.

An hour or so later, their tension had relaxed somewhat. The snowstorm, and with it the howling wind, had died away outside, the countryside was silent and beautiful under its latest mantle of snow, glistening and sparkling in the icy, silver light of the moon. Thaelmann, as hard as he was, was overcome by that old pagan feeling for the winter season. As he stood his turn on guard, he kept muttering to himself, "Oh, *wie schön . . . es weihnachtet so sehr*!"

Mallory grinned to himself as he went inside again, breath fogging on the icy air, telling himself how sentimental the Huns really were. They dearly loved all this snow, Father Xmas and the green fir trees business.

He dismissed the matter and addressed his men, sitting smoking, huddled in whatever warm clothing they had been able to find in the lonely farmhouse, obviously at peace with the world again. "Listen, we don't know what happened here. It doesn't matter. We're still too close to the front to take chances."

Silently they nodded their agreement. In the British Army's opinion they were merely a bunch of crooks who had escaped a long term inside a military prison back in 1942 because 'bodies' had been short in the Western Desert and Mallory had needed their peculiar 'talents'. All the same they were some of the best natural fighting men that the Commander had come across ever since he had been virtually blinded at the sinking of the *Bismark* and Admiral Godfrey of Naval Intelligence had ordered him to form his strange unorthodox unit. They knew the 'score', as the Yanks said. Old hands that they were, they had long known that self-discipline kept a man alive.

"We'll each take a turn at stag," he ordered. "One hour on – *outside* – that's long enough in this weather. And two hours off. We'll have reveille at zero six hundred hours."

They groaned.

Mallory smiled sympathetically, but didn't comment. He did not want to waste any further time; the more sleep they got now, the better. "If we can get an early start, I reckon we can reach the old Belgian-German frontier before it gets really light. OK?"

Again they nodded.

"All right, sort yourselves out and then we hit the hay."

Thirty minutes later they had all sunk into a heavy sleep, save for the sentry huddled in every bit of extra clothing outside, sheltered in the doorway. Now no sound disturbed the heavy silence, save the Marauders' snores and the faint hiss of the wind in the skeletal trees outside. They could well have been the last men alive in this remote wintry world. But, of course, they weren't.

"What the devil is—" Mallory caught a glimpse of a broken-nosed, brutalised face only inches from his own. He started from a heavy sleep. The stranger was peering down at him in the flickering, guttering light of one of their own candles. It threw strange, distorted, wavering patterns on the wall opposite. His nostrils were suddenly assailed by an evil stench of garlic. Opposite him, Stevens lay slumped across the back of a chair. There was blood staining the back of his yellow thatch.

Abruptly Mallory seemed to realise the danger they were in. He tried to rise. He fought the weight of the knee pressed into his chest, cursing fluently as he did so.

To no avail!

Next moment a ham-like fist smashed into his face with full force. He yelled with pain. Desperately he tried to avoid the next punch. Useless. The civilian hauled back his brawny arm once more. He laughed coarsely. The fist hit him like a pole-axe. Stars exploded in front of his eyes. Weakly he tried to fight off the red mist which threatened to swamp him. But it was no good. The last thing he saw before he passed out was Thaelmann doggedly trying to rise, the blood pouring down the side of his shattered head, while another bearded ruffian rained blows down on him with a pickaxe handle. Then Mallory was gone, his nostrils again assailed by a strange mystifying sweet cloying smell.

Four

The ancient wood-burning *Wehrmacht* trucks bumped and jolted up the winding, shell-cratered road that led from the River Moselle in the valley below. Over ruined Trier there hung the fog of war still. That night the RAF had come droning in, squadron after squadron of four-engined Halifaxes from Yorkshire and East Anglia, to drop their loads of sudden death on the old Roman city. Here and there the brown pall was ripped apart by spurts of cherry-red flame as the fires of the night flickered into life once more.

Not that the miserable prisoners in olive drab, packed tightly together in the open trucks, shivering as if in the grips of some relentless fever in the morning cold, had eyes for Trier. Even the most downcast of the American POWs told themselves the Krauts deserved all they got after what they had suffered since they had been captured. No, their red-rimmed gaze was fixed on what lay up there on the heights, waiting for them.

The Stalag (it was really a *Durchgangslager* (a transit camp) though most of the new arrivals didn't know that yet) was typical of hundreds of similar POW camps that criss-crossed the Greater German Reich in this winter of 1944. Next to the semi-ruined infantry barracks, naturally called the 'Adolf Hitler Kaserne' – they all were, it was several acres of frozen mud, shaped in the form of a hexagon by triple wire fences. These fifteen-foot high fences, electrified of course, were dominated by stork-legged wooden towers, each capped at the moment by white, frozen snow and containing elderly reservists and convalescents from the front, armed with binoculars and Spandau machine guns.

If anyone crossed the 'Death Zone' marked below they would shoot to kill immediately. If they failed to do so, they knew they would be on their way to the dreaded Eastern Front within the next twenty-four hours. Fierce Alsatian dogs, bushy-furred and half-wild, padded up and down the inner fences, tied to a long chain. If any would-be escaper managed to escape the fire of the guards, they were trained to go for the POW and spring at his throat – or testicles.

Inside the hexagon there were four neat lines of wooden huts, built on piles, Horowitz observed. He knew why. It made it easier for the German guards to probe beneath them with their long metal rods for contraband and attempts to start a tunnel. But from what Horowitz had seen of his fellow prisoners and others, captured in the Ardennes, on their way to the Trier Stalag, he didn't think many of them were in an escaping mood. Most of them, frozen, hungry, dejected by the sudden dramatic change in their lives, were simply hanging on.

Brigadier-General Horowitz sighed hard and felt another twinge of pain in his wounded foot. "What a crock o' shit," he said to no one in particular. "Brother, what a snafu!"

Further down the little convoy in a crowded half-track taken off some raw *panzergrenadiere* from a newly formed People's Grenadier Division at pistol point, Schulze and his wizened-faced running mate, Corporal Matz, were, on the contrary, in a happy mood. "Did you see all that lovely gash?" Schulze exclaimed as he finished waving to a group of 'Grey Mice', female Army auxiliaries, they had just past. "I could eat all of it without the aid of a spoon. God, man, I've got so much ink in my fountain pen that I don't know who to write to as soon as we deliver these cardboard Ami soldiers."

"Yer," Matz agreed, his usual sour look vanished, "seems a shame that they'll be playing with the five-fingered widow for the next few months, while we are generously donating our prime SS salamis to the womanhood of the Reich – God bless 'em."

"God bless 'em indeed," Schulze said enthusiastically, grabbing the bulging front of his baggy, oil-stained grey pants. "I could conduct a concert better than Karajan with his shitty little wand with what I've got inside my pants, I can tell yer, *Kumpel!*"

Listening to the two old hares through the open door of the great rumbling half-track's cab, von Dodenburg smiled. He too felt a sense of relief that they had reached the comparative safety of Trier on the other side of the Moselle. The main staging post for the Ardennes offensive was still under heavy Allied aerial bombardment – the 'air gangsters' came both at day and at night – but he and his handful of survivors from Wotan could live with that. Naturally, sooner or later, the Sixth SS Panzer Army would reach out its greedy claws to reclaim them. But he'd worry about that when the time came. Von Dodenburg's hard face, worn and fine-honed by the hard fighting of the last week, broke into a careful smile. For the average front swine, a couple of days out of the firing line seemed like heaven on earth. He nodded to the driver to slow down even more. They were approaching the gates to the *Durchgangslager*.

Carefully Horowitz eyed the pale-faced, skinny POWs streaming out of their huts on to the parade ground to welcome the newcomers. They were admittedly very thin and many of them wore *Wehrmacht* blankets over their heads to keep out the biting cold like old crones. Some were even clad in wooden shoes like French sabots instead of their combat boots. All looked pretty beat as if they didn't have a spark of resistance left in them. They were simply sitting out the war, he told himself, until they were finally released from captivity.

As the SS officer who had brought them to the camp, a tough-looking bastard with the arrogant look that seemed common to all front-line SS officers, exchanged salutes with a portly, bespectacled middle-aged officer who was probably the camp commandant, a bunch of scruffy guards came out of the guardhouse, unslinging their rifles fussily to take charge.

Horowitz took careful stock of them and the commandant, who was making ponderous, presumably self-important conversation with the SS colonel, who was nearly half his age. The camp staff didn't seem much of a problem for any would-be escaper. They were on a cushy number here and they'd obviously tried to protect their position in this relatively safe backwater. But he couldn't see them being over-zealous if an escaper tried to put up a fight. As they used to say in the 'All Americans', 'we'd rather fuck than fight.' They looked that type – in spades.

As they started to drop stiffly from the trucks, the POWs surged around them, gesturing, asking questions, shouting, "Anyone here from the 28th Div . . . Any of you guys from the Golden Lions?" and the names of a half-dozen US outfits which had suffered in the first days of the German surprise attack in the Ardennes.

Horowitz held back, feeling strangely out of place. It wasn't just the fact that the POWs were all enlisted men and he was an officer. It was the odour of defeat that emanated from them. At first sight, as he looked around at their unshaven faces and at the motley bits and pieces of uniform and civilian clothing they wore, so that they looked like a bunch of the ragmen he remembered from the New York Jewish street pedlars of his youth, it didn't seem that a single one of them would be interested in escaping. It was that which cut him off from them, he told himself.

A sergeant-major strutted up, proudly bearing the War Service Cross, Second Class on his pouting chest as his only decoration, apart from the Sport Medal in Bronze. "*Meine Herren*," he bellowed in traditional sergeant-major fashion and then followed the words with the English of, "Please remove yourselves to the block—"

"Go on, Sar'nt Major," a dozen voices protested. "Let's

have a mo to talk to the new guys . . . find out the latest poop."

But he was not having it. In a good-humoured manner, he pushed them back, with the aid of the middle-aged guards, who dealt with the American POWs as if they were a bunch of unruly, naughty boys. Slowly the new boys were led to the block hut, signposted in German '*Kommandantur*', where the good-humoured German NCO said, "Now, gentlemen, off with your clothes. You wash and then you will be looked at – please."

Next to Horowitz a tall rangy PFC said in a Texan accent, "What the Sam Hill does that Kraut think we are – a bunch o' dang steers?"

But the General wasn't listening. Instead, as the men began to take off their dirty uniforms, savouring the sudden warmth of the admin hut, his gaze was fixed on an American noncom leaning against the wall, watching, dark eyes unblinking, puffing thoughtfully at a stoogie – an American cigar – not one of the stinking cigarettes the guards smoked. Although the noncom seemed to be a Jew, he had a commanding air, with his calculated pose, an intimidating stare, the provocative smoking of an American cigar when all around the POWs would have given their right arm for a decent smoke. In that instant, a little excited voice at the back of the General's brain said, 'He's the guy . . . he's the one who's gonna get you out of this place, Mo . . .'

Outside, von Dodenburg went through the routine of having the prisoners signed for with more patience that he usually exhibited when dealing with 'rear-echelon stallions' like the Commandant. He saluted, shuffled his feet, bowed from the waist, exchanged a few pleasantries and when it was all finished responded to the other officer's 'German greeting' with one of his own as if it was back in the old days when he and the rest of the Black Guards had stamped down the Ost–West Allee with the bands blaring and the Berlin crowds cheering themselves hoarse.

He flung up his right arm in a tremendous salute, chin thrust out, eyes staring at some object known only to himself and cried, "*Heil Hitler, Herr Major!*" It was as if he were reporting to the Führer himself.

The Commandant beamed and after the little ceremony was over, he walked with von Dodenburg back to the half-track, where the Wotan troopers waited with growing impatience to be off to whatever delights in the way of 'gash, grab and suds', as they would have put it, that Trier offered. "I hope you don't mind, *Obersturmbannführer*, if I request the Local Defence Command to have you and your fine upstanding young men retained here for a little while. You can see," – he indicated the khaki-clad POWs milling everywhere in the compound – "we are grossly overcrowded and my guards simply cannot contend with such numbers. In case of an emergency, I would like to know that I can rely upon you and your firepower."

"*Selbstverstandlich* – certainly, it goes without saying," von Dodenburg heard himself saying, as if it was the most obvious thing in the world. "We shall be only too glad to help you in an emergency, *Herr Major*."

Schulze nudged Matz and nearly sent him flying over the steel side of the half-track. "Did you hear that, old house? The Old Man's got all his cups in the cupboard. He knows the score. By the Great Whore of Buxtehude, where the dogs piss out of their arses, with a bit o' luck and a smart CO we'll sit out the rest of this frigging war here in Trier like frigging God in frigging France . . ." He chuckled uproariously and elbowed Matz so hard that the tears came. All the same he echoed his old pal's sentiments with a choked, wheezed "Like frigging God in frigging France . . ."

Up in the camp, the newcomers were now nearly naked, as they prepared to shower. At the window outside of the room that led to the shower, Horowitz caught a fleeting glimpse of a pale-faced bespectacled German who was staring at the naked POWs. He spotted Horowitz watching him, flushed and after fiddling with his steel-framed glasses, as if that was the reason for his pausing, passed on again.

It was at that moment that Horowitz felt a slight ping on his naked back, followed by the soft noise of something dropped. The best he could on his wounded foot, now bleeding once more where the German medical orderly had ripped off the dirty bandage so that some doctor presumably could examine the wound after Horowitz had showered and was clean enough to be touched by the hands of a real '*Dokter Med*' of the Greater German *Wehrmacht*, he looked down and spotted the note at once.

Quickly he palmed it and in the confusion as the POWs milled forward, eager to get under the hot, steaming water of the handful of showers as they always did in all armies, Horowitz read the hastily scribbled note. It read: "Watch yer dick. A friend."

For a moment the General was completely puzzled.

Then he got it as he watched a GI strip off his soiled, smelly underpants to reveal his penis, complete with foreskin. The guy wasn't circumcised. Some of his fellow prisoners would undoubtedly have lost their foreskin to the surgeon's knife as a babe in arms, but much of them wouldn't have the same dark features that he had. But with his dark eyes, hooked nose and a circumcised dick, plus the absence of dogtags bearing his religion denomination, even the thickest Kraut would tumble to the fact that he was an American Jew. Soldiers, Jewish or Gentile, Horowitz knew, were protected by the Geneva Convention – the Rules of Land Warfare, but who knew now with Hitler's Third Reich about to disappear from the map of Europe what the fanatical Nazis might do? His mentor – and he could guess who he was – was taking no chances. He'd better not either.

"*Los . . . los*," the sergeant major urged him gently, when he seemed hesitant to enter the scalding hot water, "*hereinspaziert*."

Horowitz did as he was ordered. Bending low he pulled off his pants and his blood-stained long johns. The German noncom made sympathetic tut-tutting sounds when he saw them and Horowitz's wounded ankle. "*Vorsicht*," he said. "*Pass auf, Amerikaner*."

Horowitz took his advice. He bent low, putting his hands before his naked genitals as some men do when they are afraid the water is going to be too hot for them, and entered the showers under the benevolent gaze of the middle-aged German sergeant major. Outside, however, in the icy cold of the parade ground, the bespectacled German who had peered through the dirty window stood, his pale face puzzled. He had seen the gesture and the note. What was going on?

Five

Trier was dying.

Rapidly, inexorably, the old Roman imperial city on the Moselle was being eaten up by the thousands of phosphorous incendiary bombs being dropped by the RAF. Ever since the 'Führer Weather' had broken on the 21st December and the grey, overcast skies and fog which had been ideal for the surprise attack in the Ardennes on the other side of the river had been replaced by cold, crisp, blue-skied vistas, the British and American 'terror-bombers' had come time and time again. Now they were unloading yet another cargo of deadly steel eggs, followed by the fire bombs, on what was left of the riverside metropolis.

As they ventured out of their raid shelters to do what they could to help, the Wotan troopers were struck by the terrible heat like an open-handed slap from a hot, sweaty hand. The fires took their very breath away. They gasped like old men and bent double automatically.

Von Dodenburg held his hand in front of his eyes against the orange glare. Along the waterfront, lurid with the light of the flickering fires, he saw the facades of the eighteenth-century patrician houses swaying to and fro like stage drops. Every now and again, masonry and bricks came slithering down in noisy stone avalanches. Everywhere there was death and destruction – a burning, merciless chaos, hell created by the men some two kilometres above them on earth.

Even Schulze was aghast. "Sir," he cried, cupping his big paws around his mouth so that von Dodenburg could hear him above the roar of the inferno, "d'yer think it's any shitty use?"

Von Dodenburg knew the big NCO was right. What could his handful of battle-weary troopers do? Still they had to try. "Piss in yer handkerchiefs, scarf, helmet-liners – anything. Tie 'em around your mouths—" he finished in a burst of lung-churning coughing, as the smoke and drifting paper fragments which were everywhere penetrated his mouth.

"Yessir," Schulze yelled back and started rapping his own orders to the young troopers, many of them just standing rooted to the hot, cracked pavements, with their tar fillings molten and bubbling noisely. "Come on, you bunch of Bavarian currant-crappers, digit out o' the orifice, let's see what we can frigging well do." And when the young scared grenadiers didn't react immediately, he cried angrily, "*Los, Wollt ihr ewig leben, Scheisskerls?*"

That 'Move it, do you want to live for ever, you shitbags?' did it. The best they could, they urinated on whatever they could find in the way of cloth and tied the cloths around their mouths. Moments later they were moving out into the dying city, their eyes filled with terror and fear of what was to come.

Slowly, systematically they worked their way down the *Uferstrasse*. There were dead bodies everywhere. Some had been charred to the size of pygmies by the tremendous heat. Their blackened bodies were cracked with bright pink wounds where the flesh had split. Their teeth gleaming like polished ivory in their blackened, grimacing skulls, they made the young men vomit, sway, as if they might well fall down at any moment.

Schulze did not give them that chance. He showed no mercy; neither did his running mate, Matz. While von Dodenburg went ahead, kicking aside burning rubbish, stumbling over bodies, crying out for survivors, the two old hares slapped, shoved and kicked their subordinates ever forward after the CO.

They turned right at the entrance to the old *Roemerbruecke*, built on Roman piles still, and headed in the direction of the Catholic hospital in the centre. A group of panic-stricken amputees in blue-and-white striped smocks came hopping, crawling, swinging themselves along with their useless legs on wooden crutches (already smouldering), dragging those who had lost both legs on wooden trolleys towards them, crying for mercy, help, as the flames came after them. Von Dodenburg swallowed hard. He fought back the horror which threatened to overcome them. He would have loved to have vomited. But he knew he couldn't; he had to keep calm. Behind them came the blinded, feeling their way, tears streaming down their sightless faces, blundering and recoiling, each man alone in his own nightmarish world.

"Schulze," von Dodenburg heard himself shrieking, hardly able to recognise his own voice, "Get those men under cover."

"At the double, sir," Schulze yelled back and jumped out of the way of falling timbers, crackling and flaring with flame. He darted forward, crying, "Hold on, mates, we're coming . . . hold on, for the sake of God!"

Von Dodenburg and the rest went on. Buildings collapsed on both sides. Twice, 500 lb high explosive bombs slammed into the tarmac and knocked them off their feet with their blast. Another stick straddled the river, sending up huge whirling, white geysers of water. In the momentary garish light, a shocked von Dodenburg caught sight of a naked woman running towards the Moselle. Both her breasts were aflame. Charred, burned flesh was hanging off her body in ribbons. She been hit by phosphorous from an incendiary bomb. Where the pellets had imbedded themselves in her flesh, it burned and would continue to do so until the oxygen supply was out off.

The woman was hysterical, screaming, her mouth frothed. Von Dodenburg tried to grab her. She dodged him and sprang into the icy water. She waded forward till she was up to her neck in it. Von Dodenburg gave up. The poor swine would either die of exposure or burns. There was nothing he could do for her.

Indeed it seemed that there was nothing he and his troopers could do for any of them. But he knew they must still try. "You can't let 'em die just like that," someone expressed his thoughts in a desperate cry from the heart behind him. Von Dodenburg nodded. They had to keep on.

They swung round another corner in that dying city of horrors. The rows of trees which lined the street had been stripped bare by the blast. But the branches had been replaced by a horror-striking human fruit – *babies*! Human babies, blown by the blast from the nearby maternity home.

Matz, the hardest of them all, started to cry. Schulze vomited. Here and there troopers dropped their entrenching tools. They had been dead men for some time now, marked by war, unable to feel, to think of anything but death and impending death. Yet the sight of those innocent babies hanging from the shattered trees had been too much even for Wotan's troopers.

Instinctively von Dodenburg knew they couldn't go on. It was no use now. Soldiers expected suffering, to view it in all its horror, to suffer it. But not this . . . *no, not this*!

As the first mournful wail of the 'all clear' started to sound to the east of the city and one by one the great 88mm flak guns ceased firing, they broke off their search. Like exhausted farm labourers, infinitely weary after a hard day's toil in the fields trailing home, they made their way back to their billets. They seemed to see nor hear any of the terrible sights all around them in the devastated, wasted streets. They didn't want to.

A crazy dog was jumping up and down, yapping crazily on the dead body of its mistress, her skirt thrown up shamelessly to reveal her sex. When the woman didn't respond, the dog began to bark furiously and then to snap and bite at her dead face, as if determined to wake her. Already he had gouged lumps out of her cheeks and was now preparing to bite off the woman's nose. Von Dodenburg shot the dog, without even seeming to notice. They trailed on.

Here and there they stumbled over blackened corpses. Perhaps they saw them in their path; perhaps they didn't. It didn't matter. They were dead – they were all dead, zombies in their case. What did it matter?

A fat *Schupo* came towards him escorting a battered flier carrying his parachute cradled in his overalled arms as if the bundle of silk mattered. Behind him came a string of housewives, perfectly ordinary *Hausfrauen*, old and young, pretty and ugly. All shrieked and screamed, uttered terrible threats, attempting to strike the prisoner. Desperately the old fat policeman tried to ward them off, attempting to do his duty even in this nightmarish world. But he was failing badly. The women were closing in on the pilot.

He saw the SS in a rough-and-ready battle formation. Perhaps the cop assumed that they were there to restore some sort of order in the shattered town. '*Obersturm*'. He began looking at von Dodenburg, a note of pleading in his voice. He was sweating badly. Obviously he was as scared as his prisoner.

Von Dodenburg shook his head wordlessly.

"*Aber Obersturmbannführer—*" the policeman began, holding out his hand like he might have done years ago with all the power of his office behind him. Von Dodenburg brushed by.

The policeman's fat jowls trembled. Next to him the young pilot started to sob, his shoulders heaving like those of a broken-hearted child. The women closed in on them. A middle-aged woman, who seemed to be some sort of cook from her clothing, raised a cleaver. It gleamed silver momentarily in the ruddy light of the blazing building opposite. Then instants later it came flying down. The cop screamed and his arm, plus the pistol it had been holding, tumbled to the cobbles. It was the signal, or so it seemed. Wordlessly, as if they were eager to get some routine domestic task finished quickly, the women started hacking and kicking at the two men. The Wotan men trailed on.

By nine that evening, the men of SS Assault Regiment Wotan were well and truly drunk. It was not one of those normal and typical blinders that all infantrymen indulge in as soon as they're out of the line and have a chance to get at alcohol. It was instead a deliberate, determined attempt to blot out this terrible world; to put a stop to those terrible mental pictures of the nightmare which had happened this night in Trier and which had culminated with engineers bulldozing great heaps of the dead into mass graves – bomb holes mainly – and hastily covering them over with masses of brick rubble and masonry. It was as if every one, soldier and civilian, wanted to believe that the horror of that December evening had never even happened.

Now in their billets, mostly cellars underneath the still smoking piles of rubble, the only sound from above the steady tramp of the patrols from the *Volkssturm*, the German Home Guard, on the lookout for looters who would be shot on sight without even an attempt at a trial, they got drunk, steadily, doggedly, purposefully. In the cellar of County Leader Schmeer's home on the banks of the Moselle, a prime billet naturally, Schulze and Matz squatted cross-legged on a mattress in the corner. Opposite them on the floor there was a double line of bottles. The first line consisted of the local schnaps, Trester, the fiery first pressing of the grapes, the second was that of local wines, primarily Piesporter and Krover Nacktarsch, with its label depicting a naked baby's bottom.

Now the two old hares slumped on their mattress, solidly drinking their way through the two lines, using Schulze's traditional litany: "First a little one, comrade," he'd say with drunken formality to his running mate, and down a glass of schnaps with the usual appreciative gasp and some light-hearted witticism as "That ruptured my kidneys!", or "My cellarstud's melted – my God, that stuff must be frigging strong!" followed by an unusually polite "A drop o' naked arse or would you prefer the pissport, Corporal Matz?" to which Matz would reply with equal politeness, "Let us have the pissport for a change," before slugging down the remainder of his Piesporter with his Adam's apple going down his scraggy neck with the speed of an express lift.

Even the appearance of buxom *Frau* Schmeer, the fat County Leader's sex-starved wife, bearing a tray full of sandwiches, seemingly couldn't take the two NCOs' minds off what they had just seen and experienced. Bending down low so that the two soldiers had full view of her massive breasts threatening to plop out of her low-out dirndl, she simpered seductively, "And anything else that the two *Herren Soldaten* may wish for," – she fluttered her eyelashes – "they must just ask for, *gel*?"

"More booze," Schulze said thickly, not taking his eyes, half-closed as they were by now, from the bottles for one instant. "We've got plenty o' dead soldiers as it is, woman."

Reluctantly *Frau* Schmeer took her gaze off the bulge in Sergeant Schulze's trousers and automatically tucked one of her massive dugs that had popped out of her dirndl back into the dress as she rose. "Of course, dear Mr Sergeant. Immediately." She fluttered her eyelids once more. "Perhaps then you might like something else."

In his most ungallant fashion the 'Mr Sergeant' absent-mindedly farted.

In his bedroom one floor higher up, *Obersturmbannführer* von Dodenburg seemed to be in a similar despondent mood, concentrating too on the blessed oblivion that excess alcohol brings. County Leader Schmeer, fat, self-satisfied, still full of the usual 'golden pheasant'* rubbish, had given him a bottle of Martell. "Frog but good," he had boomed. "For a nation that makes love with its lips, the Froggies still know how to make a good cognac, my dear *Obersturmbannführer*. Take it, enjoy it. You deserve it after tonight." He winked mightily. "I'll send my little girl up" – naturally County Leader Schmeer had taken up residence in the big house's deepest cellar – 'I owe it to my people, von Dodenburg' – "later to keep you company. She's a nice child. A staunch member of the League of German Maidens."

But at that particular moment, von Dodenburg didn't need company. It was damnably hard living with oneself; company was the last thing he wanted. By now he was drinking straight from the bottle. He knew at the back of his befuddled mind he ought to be attending to his young soldiers – his 'greenhorns'. But he didn't have the heart. How could he explain to those eager, but innocent youngsters, most of them volunteers, aged seventeen and eighteen, that this was what war was really about. The battlefield wasn't a place of noble gestures, gallant officers and men dying heroically from clean wounds that showed no blood. No, the battlefield was a slaughterhouse in some backstreet, where no one died gallantly and the wounds were all too visible in their red gory horror: the work of a mad butcher, armed with a blunt cleaver.

He took another angry swallow of the French spirits. He didn't even feel the burn as the fiery liquid ran down his throat. Suddenly he felt like throwing up his hands in total, absolute despair like a man at the end of his tether and screaming, sobbing brokenly until he had no more tears to waste. But he knew the very next instant he wouldn't – he couldn't. He'd go on to the very end. "*Marschieren oder krepieren*," almost bitterly he said aloud the motto of SS Assault Regiment Wotan: 'March or croak.' He took

* Scornful nickname for Party officials, due to their pomp and gold braid.

another swig from the bottle and flung it against the wall where it shattered. Mesmerised, he started to watch as the brown liquid began to run down the wallpaper like old blood.

It was then that the quiet knock came at his door.

Six

Kreisleiter Max Schmeer belched heartily and patted his full, fat stomach like a doting mother might that of her adored firstborn. Despite everything this day, he had been able to tuck into a hearty meal of *Sauerbraten, Sosse und Spaetzle*, all swimming in plentiful, honest fat. And it was fat, he was thinking, that a real man needed to keep out the cold . . . Cheekily he turfed a piece of the meat out from between his gold teeth with a toothpick and added under his breath, ". . . and his pecker up."

He looked across at Martha, who was clearing away the supper things, as a good German housewife should (besides they didn't want the skinny maid to see what they ate. It only made the half-starved peasants envious). Again she was bending down, showing those great dumplings of hers, which he had so loved to fondle in his off-duty hours when he had been younger. "In the name of God, Martha," he ventured, emboldened by the plentiful food and wine of his evening meal, "you really have plenty of wood before your door. There's many a maid, half your age, who'd envy them tits o' yourn."

Freu Kreisleiter Schmeer was not amused. "You keep your shitty mind on your duties and not on my tits," she said sourly. "If you want to stuff that pathetic salami of yours into something, give the maid ten marks and let her have it. Why should I frigging well suffer?" She sniffed and tugged up the front of her dirndl, her mind still full of that exciting bulge in the front of Sergeant Schulze's threadbare trousers.

"Oh, dear Martha," he moaned, "don't be so hard on me, *Schnuggi-putzi*!"

"*Schnuggi-putzi* – my arse," she answered. "That's your problem – it never is hard."

Schneer who had always prided himself on his sexual ability looked at his wife aghast. 'Why,' he had used to boast at his local pub to his cronies, 'when they've had a bit of my best German salami, comrades, they can never get used to anybody else's. Just ain't the same fit.' "But you don't give me enough time," he protested.

"*Time!*" she snorted, her breasts trembling with the effort like jellies. "You'd need every frigging minute to the Day of the Last Judgement before *you* got hard."

Schmeer gasped as if someone had just slammed a tremendous punch into his fat gut. "What . . . what . . . what?" he stuttered, his face brick-red, his lip, still greasy from the *Sauerbraten*, trembling mightily, but in the same instant that he was just about to explode with indignation, the door opened and without knocking Heidi, the downtrodden maid with the permanent sniffle, came in to announce, "A *Hauptmann* Sturz from the camp to see you, *Kreisleiter*."

Frau Schmeer looked up sharply at the mention of the rank. "Who?" she queried hopefully.

"*Hauptmann* Sturz, *Frau Kreisleiter*."

"Oh him," *Frau* Schmeer grunted, suddenly deflated. "Four-eyed window-peeper." she added. Grumpily she got on with her chores, while the *Kreisleiter* buttoned up his flies and snapped, "All right, the two of you – clear that table. What do you think this is – *eine Judenschule*?"

A minute later *Hauptmann* Sturz entered the room, throwing up his right hand and murmuring, "*Heil* Hitler," as if it was a state secret to use the 'German greeting', before stating, "*Kreisleiter*, a matter of great importance."

Schmeer nodded in what he thought was a sage manner, the gesture of an older and wiser man who had seen it all – and then some. "Proceed," he commanded.

The 'staunch member of the League of German Maidens' flung her arms round the drunken von Dodenburg's neck and thrust her tongue into his surprised mouth. Her whole skinny girl's body seemed to be trembling with crazy kid's desire. He could feel her nipples growing erect through the thin white official blouse. Savagely she thrust her stomach into his.

"What's going on?" von Dodenburg asked foolishly, swaying slightly, as he stood there bewildered, it seemed, by this strange sudden attack on his person by a Hitler Maiden who didn't look a day older than fourteen.

She giggled. She released her grip. Before he could do anything, she fell on the bed. It squeaked rustily as if in anticipation. Surveyed by the Führer's scowling face above the bed, where once there had been a crucifix, she pulled open the buttons of her skirt. She let it fall. Impatiently she ripped off the blouse. Suddenly she was lying there on the bed in front of him, naked save for the simple white cotton knickers of a schoolgirl.

"Come on," she urged. "Don't waste time."

He loaded down at her as if he couldn't understand what she meant.

"*Los*!" She ran her hands over her breasts suggestively and then, as if an afterthought, she hooked her thumbs in the elastic of her knickers and, raising her plump little buttocks, pulled them off to reveal the thin blond thatch. "That's nice for you?" she whispered, her eyes half-closed.

"But you're only fifteen . . . sixteen." He found his speech at last.

"What does it matter – sixteen or sixty? It just means at sixteen it's tighter." She reached out. With a practised hand she undid his flies while von Dodenburg stood there stupidly. She thrust in one petite hand. Inside the dark cave of his breeches, she found what she sought so greedily. She started tugging at the flaccid penis, as if her very life depended upon its rising. Her breath came in short, hectic gasps. Despite the coldness of the room, her face was glazed rapidly with sweat. Her eyes seemed out of focus.

"Please stop . . ." he began, slurring his words, for he

was very drunk. "I don't—" The words died on his lips. She was doing it, working on his organ as if she were jerking an obstinate lever; he was getting hard!

Drunk as he was, von Dodenburg felt himself tremble. It was the sexual urge, so long restrained. It was over a month since he had enjoyed a woman, back in the time before the Regiment had moved into the Eifel to get ready for the great offensive which would win the war. "You mustn't," he warned thickly. "You're just a girl – a virgin . . . it'll hurt."

She laughed, still pumping madly at his growing erection.

"A virgin," he repeated as she started to draw him down on her.

"Yes, but *not* this year." Her voice was thick, as if she were slightly drunk, too. He could hear her breathing coming ever more hectically.

She lay down, still holding on to him. She raised her slim, long schoolgirl's legs. They formed a cradle for his muscular lean body. I think it's time to climb aboard," she said huskily. "You're ready to set sail."

"I . . . I . . ." he began. Then he lost all control of himself. What in three devils' name did it matter? What did anything matter?

He thrust into her almost angrily. She gasped with the shock. Then he was making love to her madly. The last thing he saw before he closed his eyes was the face of the Führer of the '1,000 Year Reich' gazing down at him in disapproval.

Below, *Kreisleiter* Schmeer was vaguely aware of the hectic squeaking of bedsprings above, but that was all. He was too concerned by the information that the pale-faced Captain Sturz from the *Durchgangslager* on the hill above Trier had brought him. "You say the Camp Commandant is not interested in your findings?" he said after a moment's consideration.

"*Jawohl, Kreisleiter*," Sturz answered, eyes gleaming angrily behind his pince-nez, which he affected in imitation of his idol, *Reichsführer* Himmler, head of the SS and Security Services. "The old woman has got his pants full. At the first sight of an Ami crossing the Moselle and he'll be off like a shot. He's already got his bag packed and his car filled with the gas he's stolen from the Quartermaster."

Schmeer frowned. "There are too many like him," he said sternly. His own car had been gassed up to the brim for weeks now and its boot was filled with the lost of years, including the treasures of Trier's rich synagogue, which he had helped to burn down in what now seemed another age. "The Führer is too soft. People like that should have been strung up from the nearest lamp-post months ago now, *Herr Hauptmann*."

"Yes, *Kreisleiter*," the Captain answered coldly. Ex-schoolmaster that he was, he had seen enough histrionics in children before the war to last him a lifetime and now he had finally escaped that petty world of education. He wanted actions not empty words. "So let me sum it up for you, sir. The man I suspect is about ten years older than the rest of that Ami scum. *One*!" Inwardly he cursed himself: he still could not get rid of that annoying schoolmaster's habit of listing things. He dismissed the thought and got on with his urgent business. "*Two*: he keeps himself well distanced from the rest of his fellow prisoners."

Schmeer listened, but his mind was again on Martha's tits. He wondered if she were already in bed keeping it warm for him. By God, with all that food inside, he'd show her how to dance the shitty mattress-polka if she were.

"*Three*: when the suspect was captured, a helmet was found nearby, close to where he was wounded." He opened his battered briefcase and wished he had a real front-line officer's leather dispatch pouch attached to his belt next to his pistol holster. With the briefcase he still looked like a shitting, candy-assed school teacher, he knew that. "This is a photograph of it." He handed the print to Schmeer, who really didn't want it.

"You'll see that it has the star of a one-star general. It bears the insignia of an American parachutist – that of the US 82nd Airborne Division – and more importantly the name written inside. You see on the sweat band: 'M – Horowitz'." He gave Schmeer a thin cold smile. "'M' for 'Moses' no doubt."

"You mean it belonged to a Yid?"

"*Genau, Kreisleiter*."

Schmeer looked puzzled.

Sturz saw the look. He recognised it. Hadn't he taught a couple of generations of stupid, lazy children, who had gazed at the ceiling like Schmeer was doing when asked a question as if they were expecting divine intervention at any moment? "So, let me recap, *Kreisleiter*. I think we have a Yiddish POW in the camp, who in reality is a general in the US airborne forces." He shrugged slightly. "Under normal circumstances, nothing very significant. A general thinking that a camp for enlisted men would be an easier place to escape from – though this one has a wounded foot," he added as an afterthought, – "than an OFFLAG*. But think where we are at this very moment." He smiled at Schmeer, who hadn't the slightest idea of what he meant.

"Yes, yes," Schmeer said hastily. "But pray elucidate if you would be so kind, *Herr Hauptmann*."

"This then. We're on the other side of the Moselle. Are the Amis prepared to launch a full-scale river crossing after their losses in the Ardennes? I doubt it." He lowered his voice significantly. "My guess is that they will do something dramatic, showy and not chance great losses."

Schmeer was impressed. There was more to Captain Sturz, with that pale masturbator's face of his and 'peeper's' eyes, than he thought. "What, *Herr Hauptmann*?"

"A paradrop, sir, to secure the Hunsruck Heights to the

* *Offizierslager*, i.e. Officers' Camp.

east of Trier. That's where we've got our artillery. Knock the guns out and there's little we can do with Trier's Home Guard to stop a determined water-crossing follow-up by the Americans."

Schmeer whistled softly. "You . . . you could be right." He thought of his car and the treasure and prayed to God for the first time since he had left the Catholic Church back in 1933: "*Mary, Holy Mother of Jesus, the True Saviour, spare my car . . . spare the vehicle of Thy humble servant.*" At that moment he felt he could have broken out into a fit of unstoppable crying at life's unfairness to him. He pulled himself together in time. "What is to be done?"

"This, sir. An airborne general surely would know something of this kind, don't you think, sir?"

"Yes . . . yes," Schmeer agreed hastily, his sluggish brain moving with remarkable speed now. He could see the danger to himself. Did that weak prick Sturz really think Germany could still stave off the inevitable defeat, the arse-with-ears? Still, he knew that it was dangerous to fool with such individuals. They'd sell their own mothers for the cause. He had to humour him. Hastily he added, "So if your camp commandant won't do anything, it means that you and I as loyal National Socialists have to act. Undoubtedly there'll be a medal in it for you, Captain. Such zeal must not go unrewarded." At the back of his fat shaven head a nasty, cynical little voice said, 'Yes, you ought to get the Order of the Purple Shaft right up where it hurts most.' "What do you suggest?"

"We work on the Jew, sir. And just to make sure that we don't fail, I would like to request the assistance of *Oberkommissar* Hohenfels of the Secret State Police. They say he can even get a mummy to talk."

"Hohenfels. Why, of course, just the man." Inwardly he shivered at the very thought of the old-time Gestapo man with those hairy paws of his hanging down, it seemed, to his knees. "His methods may be – er – a little unorthodox, but he'll get the job done."

Hauptmann Sturz rose to his feet and felt for his cap. "Then I shall take my leave, *Kreisleiter*, now that I have your permission to proceed." He put on his cap and saluted; it wasn't a very good salute, but the *Kreisleiter* returned it as if it were from an army commander himself. One couldn't be too careful with a mean-faced little bastard like the ex-schoolteacher. When Sturz had gone, he looked at the photo he had left behind and muttered to himself, "*Auf Wiedersehen, Ami*," and gave the photo a little wave of goodbye before wondering what had happened to the *Frau Kreisleiter*.

Seven

It was snowing again: thick, fat, wet flakes which came down in a solid sheet, as if God had decided that the time had come to blot out the miserable war-torn world below. In silence, the 'Kriegies',* as the POWs called themselves, trudged around the circuit in twos. But they didn't talk; they needed all their strength just to keep walking. Like white ghosts they kept moving, while it got progressively darker.

Inside the huts of the Trier camp, the home-made candles were already flickering, giving off their weak yellow light. Under other circumstances, Horowitz told himself, they might have looked romantic, reminiscent of the season of happiness and good will to all men – after all it was only two days to Christmas Eve. But not now. Now they seemed just to add to the miserable, forlorn atmosphere of the hilltop camp.

He dismissed the thought. Sudden excitement surged through his frozen, hurt body. He even forgot the stabbing pain in his foot for a while – it was bleeding again through the paper bandage, which was all that the harassed fairy of a German medical orderly had been able to find to tie up his wound. That didn't matter now. For he had received another note similar to the one that had warned him on the first day in the *Durchgangslager*. It was even on the same paper, a scrap torn from an illegal copy of Hitler's own paper *Der Volkische Beobachter* (Kriegies weren't allowed to possess German newspapers). On it had been

* From the German word for prisoner of war, *Kriegsgefangene(r)*.

scrawled: 'IMPORTANT! Meet me in the crapper at 1700 hrs. DESTROY!'

There had been no signature, no sign whatsoever of the message's origin. But by now the General had guessed from whom it had come – the Jewish-looking NCO he had observed on the first day, smoking the American cigar. Now he knew a little more about the man. The other Kriegies called him 'King Rat' – 'that guy's the centre of all the black market rackets in this goddam hell-hole. He'd sell his own mother – if he ever had one – typical kike,' they said contemptuously. 'Hand in glove with the frigging Commandant. I bet they frigging sleep together.'

Now as he limped through the streaming white-out of snow, General Horowitz told himself that 'King Rat' had to be the best-hated man in the whole goddam miserable camp.

He came to the 'crapper', the twenty-four seater latrine, its presence announced by the noxious stench long before he could see it in the whirling white fog. He was suddenly cautious. He had heard of such places in camps. Naturally, those queers who still had the strength on a starvation diet for sexual activity or were selling their bodies to the guards for sexual favours in exchange for grub met in such places. But other more dastardly things took place in the loneliness of the crappers, well away from the huts. Here, he had heard, 'Kangaroo Courts' met to condemn traitors, who were sentenced to be lured into the latrines and drowned in the noxious yellow mess. Here escapes were planned and tools were hidden for such escapes. In short, the crappers were the centre of highly illegal and potentially dangerous activities. As if in a sudden afterthought, General Horowitz grubbed in the soft new snow until he found what he sought – a large stone. He grabbed it, held it tight in his freezing fingers and entered the stinking silence of the latrine.

He blinked his eyes. The place was empty, it seemed.

There were piss-buckets in the huts and probably the Kriegies would only venture out here to squat bare-assed in the freezing place if it were absolutely necessary. Had the note been a trick? Suddenly his nostrils were assailed by an old familiar smell: the wonderful aroma of Camels. Ever since he had been a kid and had tried his first cigarette in the locker room at school he had loved that smell. How many times in these last years of combat had a Camel sustained him and put new life into him when he had been about all in! He cleared his throat and whispered, "Anyone there?"

"Over here – *General.*" That 'general' cut into his consciousness like a razor-sharp knife. He gasped, as towards the end of the crapper a figure detached itself from the shadows. Now he could see the bright red glimmer of a cigarette end. It was the strange sergeant.

"Did you say – General?" he asked, hardly daring to pose that frightening question, for if his identity was already known, he'd have to take measures, desperate measures, almost at once.

The NCO didn't answer his question. Instead he advanced upon a shocked Horowitz, pack of Camels extended. "Have a butt," he offered. "They tell me they're bad for your health." He laughed at some joke known only to himself.

In a daze Horowitz took one and the NCO, who had still not introduced himself, flicked his Zippo (Horowitz wondered how in Sam Hill he had managed to retain such a precious object in the camp, but he didn't ask) and the General bent to receive the proffered light. He puffed hard till the Camel glowed. Then he asked, "What's going on?"

In the growing white darkness, with the snow hissing down in sheer sheets outside, he couldn't see the other man's face. Still, he fancied he could see that its dark features were set in a cynical, all-knowing look, as if the noncom were generations older than he and knew all of man's innate weakness.

It seemed to take the other man quite some time before

he answered carefully in a whisper, as if the enemy lurked at the very door of the latrine listening to every word, "I'm the Commandant's *Vertrauensmann*. You understand?"

Horowitz did. '*Vertrauensmann*', a man of trust, was the camp inmates' representative to the commandant.

"The guys think I'm more – I'm the Commandant's spy." The noncom paused and Horowitz could imagine him pulling a wry face at the statement. "In a way the guys are right. I give the old asshole bits and pieces about the Kriegies, so he trusts me and they hate me. After all I am a kike and every decent, white, Protestant, red-blooded American knows that all kikes are two-timers."

Horowitz made no comment. Despite his cynicism, the noncom really was sensitive about his Jewishness. It hurt to be called a 'kike' and feel an outsider in his own country.

"But by gaining the Commandant's confidence, General, I get to know things – important things sometimes. Like the fact they suspect you're an American general – and of course, I *know* you are."

Horowitz stubbed out his precious cigarette a little angrily. "Just how do you know – or suppose you know – *that*, soldier?"

"I just do. But it doesn't matter what I know. I'm on your side, perhaps even more than I would be normally with a so-called fellow American. After all, you are Jewish as well."

Suddenly the General was no longer hostile. Instinctively he knew that this strange noncom who had still not given him his name was a patriot and, in his particular case, he was there to help him. "All right," he snapped, a general officer once more, used to giving commands and having them accepted, "cut the bullshit. What's going on? What do you know? How does it affect me? And if it does, how can you help me, Sergeant, eh?"

The NCO chuckled. It was a strange sound in that

stinking darkness in the heart of the enemy's camp with the snowstorm howling outside, the flakes beating on the latrine's tin roof in drumroll after drumroll, as if the beat would never cease. "Hold your horses, General," he said finally.

"*OK* . . . shoot the works, Sergeant."

"This is the deal, sir. That four-eyed bastard, whose face you must have seen by now peering through the damned windows is the camp's intelligence officer. But I wouldn't be surprised if he didn't work for one of the Krauts' other security agencies – military intelligence, the SD,* perhaps even for the frigging bullyboys of the Gestapo."

"Go on, Sergeant."

"Well, Sturz – that's his moniker – has almost nailed you, sir. I'm sure of that. The Commandant let slip to me that Sturz had been to see him about you. But he got no dice from the Commandant. That guy's creaming his drawers at this very moment. He's got his duds packed and is ready to bug out at a moment's notice. So we've nothing to fear from the Camp Commandant."

Horowitz noted the 'we', but didn't comment on the use of the plural. Instead he waited for the NCO to continue, his mind racing electrically as he considered his position and the great secret which had been entrusted to him.

"I'll give Sturz not more than twenty-four hours before he cracks down, sir. He knows that after Christmas Eve – the Krauts do go all gooey about this Christmas crap, even arseholes like Sturz – the camp is to be evacuated. They're expecting Bastogne to fall soon and the frontier will be flooded with our prisoners, or they hope it will be. So Trier is to be evacuated to Limburg up on the Rhine, leaving the place open for the new boys. Sturz knows he'll lose you once you're moved, so" – the other man paused in the darkness – "he'll crack down after Christmas Eve and the Krauts have said their dinky

* SD: the SS's own intelligence and security organisation.

poems in front of the Christmas tree and all that sentimental crap."

"You seem to know a lot about the Germans," Horowitz ventured.

The other man chuckled drily. "I should do. I was one once upon a time." He paused and Horowitz half anticipated he would explain more. But he didn't. Instead he continued with, "'Kay, sir, then we'll have to get you out before then, won't we?"

"*Get me out?!*" Horowitz exclaimed, caught completely off guard by the bald statement.

"Yeah. Christmas Eve, I thought. The guards'll be relaxed. They'll have drunk a little extra and be mooning about, singing that crappy '*Stille Nacht, Heilige Nacht*' bullshit of theirs."

Under other circumstances, Horowitz would have laughed at the hard-nosed cynicism of the other man, making fun of Kraut sentimentality – and American for that matter, too. But not now. His mind was too full of the NCO's statement. He was going to get him out. "But how?" he finally found his voice.

"I don't think it should be too difficult, General. The problem starts once you're out of this dump. It's outlaw country out there—"

"Over the Moselle?" Horowitz cut him short eagerly.

"Yes."

"Then the question is which direction . . . where can we expect the most trouble from the Krauts' rear-echelon people?" He paused briefly. "We can go north or south, not straight ahead, because that's where the bulk of the German forces attacking Bastogne will be—"

"General . . . General, sir," the NCO interrupted him firmly. "This ain't no general staff exercise. Let's get out of the goddam place and across the Moselle. I've already got that planned. There are still plenty of small boats anchored on this side of the river now all river traffic has been stopped – courtesy of Allied air forces. Then we'll consider which way we go from there."

"Yes, of course, of course, you're right. We'll play it by ear." He paused again. "I take it from your words that you're coming with me, which will be a help with my goddam foot."

"Yeah, General, I'm coming with you – and it's not only on account of your foot, sir." The other man's voice in the white darkness suddenly grew very solemn. "I've gotta get out of here soon . . . I might not have a chance later." He emphasised the 'later', as if he already knew that something bad was due to take place.

"How do you mean – later?" Horowitz answered.

He received no answer, for suddenly the other man seemed to be in a great hurry. An instant later, Horowitz knew why. He could hear the harsh, hurried crunch of someone coming through the snow, heading for the latrines, as if he had been taken short by a sudden emergency.

"Someone's got the squitters," he said, trying to be funny and lessen the sudden tension. But he could sense he was having no effect. The NCO was listening hard, almost fearfully, to the approaching footsteps, as if they heralded some kind of danger.

"I'm off," the other man whispered urgently. He fanned the air to get rid of the smell of the good American tobacco. "Don't tell anybody of this or our meeting. Better that way. I can't trust anybody. So long . . ." His voice vanished. Horowitz heard the slither of feet and next instant he disappeared into the shadows from whence he had come.

Not a moment too soon. The length of hessian which attempted (and failed) to keep the cold out of the crapper was thrown back hastily. A figure entered. He was panting hard and Horowitz could sense the man was fumbling urgently with his pants.

"If there's anybody in here," a Texan voice proclaimed breathlessly, "prepare to receive green smoke . . . 'Cos my guts are about to fall apart." The Texan plumped himself down on the freezing wooden seat of the crapper and promptly did what he had just proclaimed he would. Horowitz, whose sense of smell was sensitive at the best of times, didn't even notice. His mind was racing joyously with what was to come. Outside the snow continued to fall in a solid white sheet.

Eight

"Come on, you sow-heap!" Schulze cried, breath fogging the icy air of the snowbound schoolyard, "*Att – ention!*"

As one, two hundred pairs of jackboots clicked to attention and the set, rigid faces of the survivors of SS Assault Regiment Wotan stared at some far horizon known perhaps only to themselves.

Von Dodenburg waited till Schulze, the senior NCO still alive, swung round and marched towards him through the frozen snow to report. Even though his head was thick and his vision a little shaky after the night's indulgences, he could see what a splendid bunch his young survivors were; the best that National Socialist Germany could produce in this fifth year of war. All of them were well over one metre eighty and each and every one of them was a volunteer. If they were no longer perhaps ready to die for their Führer, as their fanatical predecessors had been in the years gone by, they were still prepared to fight to their last breath for Wotan and Germany. All of them, even the most stupid, knew that Germany's fate was sealed if they and thousands like them did not make the enemy pay an impossible price for victory.

"SS Wotan all present and correct, sir," Schulze barked, as if they were still on the *Leibstandarte*'s parade-ground at Berlin-Lichtenfeld. He winked.

Von Dodenburg frowned, but not severely. The discipline which existed in Wotan these days was not that of the old days, the 'Cadaver Obedience', as they used to call it, born of fear and harsh punishment. Now in December 1944 Wotan existed on the basis of mutual confidence, a kind of blood brotherhood and comradeship engendered by self-sacrifice and the willingness even to die for a pal if necessary. "Thank you, *Oberscharführer*."

"Sir." Schulze swing round on his heel in a flurry of snow. He puffed out his enormous chest and cried, the air jetting in twin grey streams from his nostrils like that of a hard-worked nag, "Wotan – stand at ease . . . Stand easy."

As one, the men shot out their right feet and folded their hands in front of their stomachs in the position of 'stand easy'.

Von Dodenburg wasted no time. It was freezingly cold on the open yard, with the black, charred skeletons of the bombed-out eighteenth-century houses all around. There wasn't a soul in sight. It was as if Trier had been bombed out of existence, though von Dodenburg did notice a thin plume of wood smoke spiralling upwards from *Kreisleiter* Schmeer's house. He, at least, would never go cold; the big shots always won out whatever the circumstances.

"*Morgen Soldaten*!" he cried the traditional greeting.

"*Morgen Obersturmbann*," a couple of hundred throats thundered back lustily.

Von Dodenburg smiled. His young troopers were still in good heart despite everything they had suffered since that momentous Saturday.* "Comrades, I have some good news for you all."

Schulze looked puzzled. Von Dodenburg never knowingly bullshitted the men, he knew, but some officers did. Was there a hidden trap in this supposed good news?

Next moment, he knew differently and realised once again that the interests of Wotan's ragged-assed stubble hoppers were always uppermost in the Old Man's mind. For von Dodenburg continued with, "I have just received a signal from higher headquarters" – he flashed his harsh hard smile at them for a moment – "that we are to stay here and bolster

* Saturday 16th December 1944, when the great surprise German offensive in the Ardennes commenced.

up the local *Volkssturm*. They are not the most elite of troops as you know and up there on the hill there are a thousand or so able-bodied Ami prisoners in the camp who might break out if their people on the other side of the Moselle attack, which is very likely sooner or later. The Amis couldn't present a greater danger than at this moment."

Matz farted contemptuously and said to no one in particular, "Amis, I've shat 'em . . . A bunch of frigging wet-tails, if I ever saw 'em."

Von Dodenberg allowed himself another smile at the remark. "So," he continued, "what does that mean?" He answered his own question. "This. It means we shall be spending Christmas Eve and presumably long—"

Von Dodenburg never finished his sentence. His words were interrupted by a tremendous, heartfelt cheer that sent the rooks rising from the roofs and shattered buildings all around in hoarse, cawing protest. "Heaven, arse and cloudburst!" Schulze cried above the sudden outburst of wild excited cheering. "Ain't yer off yer mother's tit yet? . . . Don't you shitty Christmas tree soldiers know you're on shitty parade?" But at that particular moment no one was listening, not even to Senior Sergeant Schulze, feared for his tongue and his Hamburg Equalizer* throughout the whole of the SS.

Von Dodenburg waited patiently till the cheering had died down before saying, "All right, Sergeant Schulze, you can dismiss this rabble. Tell them to start learning their Christmas Eve poems straight off." He lowered his voice, "See then that a recon party is sent out to see what it can find for a poor soldiers' Christmas."

Schulze winked knowingly. He knew what the CO meant. Beneath the ruins of Trier, there would be cellars filled with wine and spirits. After all, Trier was the capital of the local booze industry. There'd be plenty of 'suds' and 'firewater'

* Schulze's famed set of polished brass knuckles, inherited from his docker father and his father before him.

buried under the still smoking rubble to keep Wotan happy for several Christmases, he was certain. He swung von Dodenburg a tremendous salute, his right hand quivering mightily with the smart motion and then bellowed out his orders. The men streamed away happily, chatting excitedly among themselves, young minds already full of the exciting festive days to come, far from the firing line and that fate they had lived with for weeks, months now – 'Bite the shit and spend the rest o' your days looking at the taties from below', as Schulze would have put it in his own inimical style – DEATH!

Von Dodenburg relaxed and watched as they set off on their various tasks, looking for all the world like a bunch of excited schoolboys abruptly released from a boring lesson, before beckoning for his two senior NCOs, Schulze and Matz, to approach him. "All right," he said without wasting time – it was too cold for that, "I don't have to draw you a picture. We'll use the golden pheasant's house" (he meant Schmeer's) "as our HQ. Matz, you'll establish a command post up in one of those bunkers on the lower hills of the Hunsruck. There are plenty of abandoned *Westwall* fortifications up there."

Matz pulled a face. "Freeze the old waterworks up nice and sharp up there," he protested.

"Just go through the motions, Corporal Matz. And if anyone knows how to blind 'em with bullshit, it's you. Put up a couple of radio aerials, a flag and repair the barbed wire. That should do it and—"

"And then do a bunk down here again right damned smartish, sir?" Matz interjected, brightening up immediately.

"Correct in one, Matz. Then you, Schulze, and you too, you little rogue, I want you to organise the Christmas festivities. This is going to be one wartime Christmas that those young troopers are never going to forget even if they live to be granddaddies." He frowned. Naturally none of them would. SS as they were, belonging as they did to the *Waffen SS*'s premier regiment, 'the Führer's Fire Brigade', as

Wotan was called throughout the *Wehrmacht*, it was hardly likely they'd live to see their majority, never mind their three score and ten.

He dismissed the thought as soon as it had come and concluded with, "All right, you two rogues, set to it." He shot a glance at his watch. "We've got exactly thirty-six hours till Christmas Eve. We can anticipate that the Anglo-American air terrorists will bomb twice again in that time – at least – but by sixteen hundred hours on Monday 24th December in the year of Our Lord 1944, I want the Christmas trees up, the presents and the booze ready and our boys safely in the cellars ready for—"

"The biggest piss-up in the history of Wotan, sir," Matz cried joyfully.

"Bring on the dancing girls," Schulze chortled, "though God knows what these cardboard soldiers of ours would do with a real-life piece of juicy female gash!"

Von Dodenburg shook his head in mock wonder at the exuberance of the two old hares before turning and crying over his shoulder, "Thirty-six hours remember." With that he disappeared into the house, his mind buzzing with his own plans for what he knew would be the last Christmas of World War Two.

Two kilometres away on that wind-swept hill, Horowitz and the strange sergeant with the German accent (for since their second meeting the General had discovered that Tech/Sgt Joe Rosenstein had been born not a hundred miles from this very spot in Frankfurt-am-Main) sheltered behind the cookhouse, savouring the warmth that occasionally came from it when someone opened the door. Not a dozen yards off, the Russian POWs, who did the dirty jobs in the camp like cleaning the latrines and laying out the dead (and there were plenty of them), were scavenging among the potato peelings for chunks of raw potatoes that had been overlooked by the US hash-slingers.

Rosenstein, his dark eyes searching the dreary landscape

ceaselessly, said out of the side of his mouth like some Hollywood B-movie hood, "Sturz, the security guy, is a faggot of course, General. I suppose guys like that are naturally attracted to places like this. You know, scoutmasters and scouts sort of thing."

Horowitz, shivering in the cold, nodded, not very interested. Still the ex-German Jew had asked him here for a purpose, so he listened.

"Now and again he hits the jackpot and finds one of our guys who'll play with him in the crappers for a meat sandwich or a piece of that sausage of theirs. You know, sir, the younger guys feel completely in his power – and besides, the poor bastards are at near starvation."

"Yes, I understand. I don't like it, Rosenstein, but I don't condemn it. So what is it to us?"

By way of an answer, Rosenstein straightened to his full height and pulled a pair of glasses out of his pocket. They were a pince-nez. Carefully and somewhat pedantically he placed them on the bridge of his nose and cleared his throat like a schoolmaster about to address his class. "*Guten Morgen, junge Herren*," he began and then gave a surprised Horowitz one of his rare and very careful smiles. "Ring a bell, sir?"

"*Hauptmann* Sturz – well almost. The glasses did it.

"Exactly, sir. So what's the drill? I'll tell you, sir."

Under other circumstances Horowitz would have smiled. Rosenstein was one of these typical Central European Jews – he'd met a lot of them as emigrés before Pearl Harbor. They had not been the slightest bit intimidated by their change of circumstances; that they were foreigners in a foreign land. They were Jews, weren't they, among Jews? That was enough, eh? So Rosenstein talked to him, a one-star general, as if they were on equal footing. But it didn't matter. Here he needed Rosenstein with his know-how and perfect German. So he listened.

"*Herr Hauptmann* Sturz is going to be our key to get out of this damned place." He smiled at the startled General.

"But how? . . . Why?" Horowitz stuttered, caught completely off guard.

Opposite, two of the ragged Russians, unshaven beneath their moth-eaten fur caps, were rolling in the snow, fighting, biting, cursing as they struggled for a large piece of blackened raw potato. "*Davoi*!" Rosenstein called as if annoyed. "*Los hau ab*!" The Russians continued to fight.

"Why, you ask, sir? Rosenstein continued, trying to ignore the struggle now that his commands had been to no avail. "I shall tell you." He puffed himself up and extended one hand like a conjuror about to produce a rabbit from an empty silk hat to the amazement of his audience of admiring children. "Because *I* shall be *Hauptmann* Sturz."

Hastily he filled in the details of his bold plan while Horowitz listened with rapt attention, his admiration for Rosenstein's ingenuity unbound now until, when the Sergeant paused for breath, he was finally able to put in a quick question. "When?"

Sergeant Rosenstein, formerly of Frankfurt-am-Main, scion of a family that traced its roots to the medieval Fuggers and to the Marxes who had lived not a mile from where the two plotters crouched at this very moment, smiled proudly and announced, as if he were addressing a mass audience, "Why, on that night devoted to sweetness and light and goodness to all men – *Christmas Eve*!"

In the churned up snow and mud, the bigger of the two Russians was choking his opponent to death, the precious hunk of raw potato gripped between his stainless steel false teeth. Horowitz didn't even notice.

PART THREE

Treachery at Trier

One

"Come on," General Gavin said urgently, as they clambered into the little convoy of jeeps waiting in the yard of his barracks HQ in Vielsalm, the drivers gunning their engines impatiently, "while this goddam snow holds off." He nodded to his jeep driver, huddled in a parka, as he and Mallory clambered into the open jeep. Mallory and his Marauders had been forced to return to Vielsalm to recover after a narrow escape. In the seat next to the driver, the 82nd Airborne commander's bodyguard pulled up his tommy gun. He needed to: since the survivors had abandoned the salient behind St Vith, the Germans were pressing forward everywhere. Already they had their scouts and reconnaissance parties lurking in the snowbound woods to both sides of Vielsalm.

Gavin's driver didn't wait to see if Mallory's Marauders had piled into the follow-up jeep. He crashed home first gear, gunned the engine once more – hard – and set off. He didn't want to risk the General's anger by stalling the little vehicle in the freezing morning temperature.

They swung out of the barracks, started to climb the slick slope leading out of the little town and began heading along the dead-straight country road leading to Werbomont some dozen miles away. While they dodged in and out of the nose-to-nose traffic also heading west, the trucks packed tight with exhausted survivors, the General shouted into Mallory's ear, "Let me explain, Commander. We've get some 20,000-odd men coming out of the salient since yesterday morning. About five per cent of them are wounded, with about another five hundred seriously so. They've got to have surgery back in Louvain, Brussels, perhaps for all I know in the UK as well."

Mallory nodded his understanding. The handsome paratroop commander looked worried, very worried. It was natural. Not only was he responsible for holding the advancing Hun, he was, too, for these exhausted survivors and their wounded. The US Army didn't like the idea of giving up ground, even less that of suffering a high number of casualties. It didn't look good in the headlines back in the States; and in 1944, Mallory knew, US generals were highly sensitive about their public image. With their PR nicknames, such as 'Iron Mike', 'Wild Bill' and all the rest, they were like a bunch of prima donnas. Not Gavin, he told himself. He was a combat general who led from the front; he was concerned about the ordinary GI and his suffering.

"So it's my priority number one this morning to get those seriously wounded out now. Driver, watch those GIs. You nearly ran the poor bastards down – after what they've suffered."

"Sorry sir," the harassed young jeep driver said and swerved wildly. Mallory clung on for dear life and waited for the General to continue.

"Now I'll show you how it is done. Risky but effective we've found in the past. It's quick, however, and in this kind of weather," – he indicated the snow clouds building up to the east once more – "it's one way of beating it. If the dawn snow comes again it can take hours, perhaps even days to get out of these hills and down to the North Belgian plain on the other side of the River Meuse."

"I see, sir," Mallory said, but in fact he didn't. What had the wounded of the battered 106th and 7th US Divisions got to do with their rescue attempt? But he didn't object. He had learned – the hard way, for a man of his quick-fuse temper and impatience with bullshit – to let the brass have their head. Rank had its privileges.

"We developed the method in Sicily last year. It worked in Normandy and Holland, though in all those three cases,"

Gavin went on, "the climate, the season and the terrain were all different. Let's see how it works in the Ardennes in the middle of a damned cold winter." And with that he fell silent, brooding on problems known only to himself, while the driver sped, the best he could, up the road towards Werbomont and whatever lay there for the Marauders to see.

Behind them in the follow-up jeep, Spiv commented scornfully, "Look at them frigging Yanks, I've shat better soldiers for brekker."

Thaelmann, his long nose purple with the cold and dripping sadly like a leaky tap, looked at the skinny soldiers with their poor physique, who looked as if their very rifles were too heavy for them as they drudged through the slush and ice miserably. "Typical products of the capitalist system," he opined in his harsh accent, "ground down by poverty and poor wages."

"Come off it, Thaelmann," Peters said, "poor sods have been through a hard time, that's all. You'd look like that, if you'd been through what they had."

Thaelmann wasn't impressed. With a stereotypically German lack of feeling, he replied, "There are no excuses for the failings of the capitalist system. When the war is over, it will be our duty to convince them that there is only one way ahead – *communism*!" Suddenly he looked very proud and challenging.

At that moment, the driver applied his brakes sharply and the jeep shimmied wildly for a moment on the slick icy surface of the *pavé* before the cursing, sweating driver finally brought it under control and the Marauders were able to see what had caused the sudden halt.

To their right a level stretch had been cleaned of snow and there stood three Waco gliders, well spaced out with some two hundred yards or so between each one. Around them, aidmen busied themselves carrying in stretcher after stretcher of seriously wounded GIs, with those who could still walk hopping forward supported by other medics, and here and there by women Army nurses, muffled in parkas and khaki overcoats, so that it was only their waddle which identified them as women.

"Lovely grub," Spiv chortled and Kitchener's eyes sparkled at the sight. But the other occupants had no eyes for the handful of plain US Army nurses; their gaze was fixed on the gliders, each one of them wondering what purpose the engineless gliders could serve in the evacuation of the seriously wounded.

Gavin didn't take long to enlighten them. Standing to one side on a small hillock on the side of the road to Werbomont so that they would not be in the way of the seemingly endless stream of boxlike ambulances moving to and fro, he said to Mallory and his Maranders, "You see those two poles about a couple of hundred feet in the front of the leading Waco?"

They nodded and Mallory eyed the two poles, both hurriedly prepared pine trunks from the nearby forest and each one surmounted by a battery-powered blue light that probably, Mallory told himself, could only be seen by someone searching for it deliberately from above.

"Now watch what's going to happen."

Even as he spoke, a half dozen men in the high lace-up boots of his paras took the glider tow rope fixed in the nose of the little Waco and started dragging it to the left-hand pole. One of them – a black guy – shinned expertly up the rough pole with the tow rope over his shoulder, while Spiv sneered, "I allus told yer them darkies had tails."

Mallory frowned at him significantly and the little ex-barrow boy shut up abruptly, as if he had suddenly lost the power of speech.

The black 'All American' pulled the heavy rope over the top of the left-hand pole and then, balancing himself the best he could – almost like a circus acrobat, he lunged forward dangerously and pulled it forward over the other pole. That done he dropped it far enough for his comrades to reach up and pull it to the ground before doubling back to the Waco with it.

Mallory's look of bewilderment grew. What the hell were the Yankee paras up to? And how was this complicated rigmarole going to be of use to him and his Marauders?

But for a moment or two Gavin was not forthcoming. He was watching the men intently, as if it was very important that his paras did the job, whatever it was, correctly. Now there was the low throb of an aeroplane's motors coming from the west. But all of them were too intrigued by what was going on in front of them to take much notice.

By now the paras had dragged the heavy tow rope back to the nose of the glider where now a pilot had taken his seat behind the wide expanse of the fogged-up Perspex of the cockpit. Behind him the ambulance-men and the stretcher-bearers had finished their task and were taking a breather. They had filled the Waco with stretchers and seriously wounded.

The sound of the aircraft engines were getting louder now. They had closed the door of the Waco. On both sides of the tow rope the paras had taken it up on command and were bracing it more tightly, pulling in the slack. Somewhere further off a green flare soared into the grey, leaden sky and exploded there. It bathed the strange scene in its unreal, incandescent light.

"Now watch," Gavin ordered the puzzled spectaters. "Tricky, but swell when it works."

Even as he spoke, the C–47 'Dakota' had broken from the low cloud and was coming straight for them. It flashed its recognition signal. Mallory watched as the para officer on the ground flashed back his acknowledgement with his own signal lamp.

Even with the roar of the C–47's twin engines, Mallory could hear the rush of air as the Waco's brakes were released. Up on the strange poles the blue lights had begun to burn.

Up above, the C-47 had throttled back with an ear-splitting roar. "What in Christ *is* going on, sir?" Spiv yelled. But everyone, including Mallory, was too mesmorised by the scene before their eyes to explain – that is, if they could have done.

Now just above stalling speed, the big military transport came in. Everywhere necks were craned. White faces stared upwards. Most were merely curious; these in the know, however, looked anxious. They knew of old that this was the moment of truth. If anything went wrong, the wounded inside the Waco wouldn't stand a cat's chance in hell.

Next to Mallory, Gavin bit his bottom lip with suppressed tension.

Up above, with the C-47's silver bulk filling, it seemed, the whole sky, a steel hook was lowered beneath its tail fin. A steel boom carrying it came lower. It began to dawn on Mallory what the daring manoeuvre was that the pilot was about to carry out. He too bit his lip with tension. He felt the coppery taste of blood in his mouth.

The C-47 came growling in at tree-top height. The prop wash lashed up the snow of the field into a white fury. The plane seemed so low that it appeared to be skimming the field in a silvery haze. Surely it had to crash in a second. No one could pilot a plane successfully at that altitude!

Clank! There was the hollow sound of metal striking metal. The Waco troubled violently, so much so that it seemed that the frail canvas and wood craft might fall apart at any moment.

Above, the snatch plane staggered visibly. Gavin and Mallory held their breath, tense with worry and excitement. Gavin had seen it happen before that the impact had been too much for the C-47 snatch plane. It had come hurtling to the ground with no height to be gained, smashed into smithereens in a great ball of violet light.

The sudden jerk was taken up by the nylon tow rope. The hook caught in the rope. It snatched the tow rope off the tops of the poles. "Christ Almighty," Spiv gasped, "get a load of that, Kitch, will yer?" The plane's twin engines roared mightily. The plane's pilot was using full power now. "Come on, come on," Gavin yelled in a strained voice, digging his fingernails cruelly into the palms of his hands. Up above, the pilot rammed his throttles forward. The engines thundered in anguish. He lifted the C-47's nose. It was now or never!

The glider jerked. It was as if sudden life was surging through its frail structure. It started to rise. In an instant it was snatched from 0 to 80 miles an hour. It was moving . . . moving. "Hell's bells!" Peters gasped in his thickest Geordie accent. "Now that's reet canny, ain't it?" But no one was listening. They had eyes and ears solely for the glider as it began to ascend shakily into the air, rising higher and higher by the second.

A ragged cheer broke out from the weary medics and those of the waiting wounded, who were still conscious, as the glider vanished towards the west, getting smaller and smaller by the minute until it finally vanished into the low cloud over the River Meuse.

Slowly, his shoulders bent slightly, as if he were abruptly very weary, Gavin turned to Mallory. "Well, Commander, what you think?"

Mallery shook himself like a dog does when it awakes from some doggy nightmare. "Very impressive, sir, very impressive indeed." He pulled himself together, telling himself that the glider snatch from the ground showed typical Yankee 'get-up-and-go', but that, for the life of him, he could not see what it had to do with him and his Marauders.

The handsome Airborne General in his immaculate uniform and gleaming, polished jump boots forced a grin. "You're wondering, aren't you, of course, what the damned Sam Hill this has got to do with you and your particular problem?"

Mallory nodded a little warily and answered, "Yes, I am sir."

"Well let's get back to HQ in Vielsalm and I shall tell you." Without another word he turned and marched across the slushy field to the jeep where the young driver was already gunning his engine once more, as if he could read his boss's mind.

Two

The GI wiped a dirty hand, finger nails caked in muck across his thin, unshaven face. He looked just about at the end of his tether. "What am I doing here?" he asked rhetorically. "Two months ago I was a goddamn short-order cook, a simple hash-slinger in Metz, now I'm a frigging rifleman in the middle of frigging nowhere."

Mallory smiled sympathetically. Behind his back as they crouched in the snow-heavy fire, with the guns rumbling ominously in the background, Spiv sneered to 'Gyppo', as he called the Egyptian. "Pass me yer snot rag, will yer? I'm gonna breakdown and blub."

Mallory and the weary front-line ex-cook turned infantry scout ignored the comment. Instead Mallory asked, "What's in front of us, soldier, as far as you know?"

"Krauts," came the bald answer. "Plenty of the bastards. Hundreds . . . thousands of the frigging assholes."

Mallory tried to ignore the fact that the GI was about to cry; there was a wet sheen across his bloodshot eyes that indicated he was close to tears. "I understand. But could you tell me the path you took? You got back safely. Perhaps that would help."

"It's your funeral, brother," the GI said. "'Kay, this is the deal."

Five minutes later they set off into what the frightened GI had called 'outlaw country', for it was nearly a week now since the Germans had conquered this part of Luxembourg close to the German frontier. Fortunately they needed most of their fighting troops up near Bastogne and the Meuse and Mallory reasoned that they might be lucky enough to get through the enemy's second-rate supply troops without too much trouble until they finally reached the spot where the River Sauer flowed into the Moselle. There, there was likely to be more German activity. But, he told himself, as they progressed steadily through the wooded rugged heights above the Sauer, he'd worry about that particular problem when he came to it.

Now it was almost darkness. The silence which followed the last German artillery barrage of the day had taken on a new quality, Mallory couldn't but help feel. It had a strange brooding feel about it. It gave him the sensation that there was someone – something – just behind him. Twice he resisted the temptation to look in that direction – but the third time, he did so. Naturally there was nothing there save their footprints in the snow, glittering in the spectral light of the half moon.

It had cleared now. The velvet night sky was ablaze with the hard silver rays of a myriad stars. To the east there was a lot of activity he noted, too. Flares shot into the sky all the time. But he found them encouraging. The guards at the German supply dumps to the east were nervous, that was all. It was a sign that they were second-class troops, who should provide them with little trouble if they bumped into them, which he didn't want.

They skirted an abandoned hamlet. It was in ruins and already the snow had piled up on the shattered humble cottages and occasional farm. Not even some abandoned dog howled at the moon. The place, it was obvious, had been empty since the start of the German attack. Another good sign.

They came across a hastily left behind US trailer, packed with soaked K-rations. They weren't even worth looting. But the cigarettes and candies had gone. The Germans had passed this way already, but again that had probably been back on that fateful Saturday 16th December. It was growing cold now with the freezing wind straight from Siberia sweeping across the snow plain and Mallory would have dearly liked to stop in the shelter of the ruined hamlet. But he knew that wasn't possible. He wanted to be in position at the confluence of the Sauer and Moselle by dawn. He ordered his little group of Marauders to keep on going.

It was five minutes later that Peters in the lead stopped dead, crouched low, head moving slowly from side to side, US grease-gun at the ready, searching his front.

The others moved forward, still keeping their distance from one another like highly trained troopers. Automatically, without orders, they formed a small defensive perimeter to left and right of the forest track, while Mallory edged closer to Peters, carbine at the ready, and bending close to the ex-guardsman, asked in a careful whisper, "What do you see?"

"Hear, sir," the other man whispered back. "At three o'clock, sir. Just to the right side of that clump of firs. Got it?"

"Got it, Peters," Mallory answered and using the old soldier's trick, he bent and then raised his head slowly, sweeping from left to right. In this manner the observer would see any slightly lighter object outlined against the darker background, especially if the object moved.

He stopped short. A shadow *had* detached itself from the darker shadow of the group of firs to his right. There was someone there. Next instant he heard a faint whistling like that of a man happy with himself, going about his tasks (whatever they might be) in this midnight wilderness, as if he hadn't a care in the world.

"Germans?" Peters hissed.

Mallory hesitated. There seemed something vaguely familiar about the tune the unknown man was whistling. Then he had it. Indeed so surprised he was at the act of recognition that Mallory almost started whistling it himself. It was that old French *poilu* marching song for World War One. Under his breath, he lilted a few words of it: "*Auprès moi ma blonde . . .*"

Peters pressed his mouth so close to Mallory's ear that the latter could smell the odour of ham and chicken from the K-ration he had eaten at their last break. "Is he OK, sir?" he hissed.

"I think so," Mallory began, "he's singing in French so he's not a Hun—" He stopped abruptly. Hadn't he and the others thought the same when they had been trapped in the lonely house in what now seemed another age, chloroformed and out to the world until they had been brought round and told by their bearded, evil-looking captors that they had fallen into the hands of the '*Armée Blanche*', the Belgian White Army?

At first they had believed the supposed partisan leader. He looked the part, despite that crooked smile and greedy drunk's eyes. He wore the white overalls of the Resistance movement and carried a Sten gun, of British origin. He was effusively apologetic for having them knocked out and drugged. He had fed them a hot meal with plenty of good Stella Pils to wash the food down. Yet there had been something about the man and his followers with their staring eyes, following every move that their former captives made as if their very lives depended upon it, which had repelled him, made him suspicious.

It had been a good thing he had been so suspicious. After they had broken out and fled for their lives, followed by a fusilade of angry Sten gun fire, they had discovered that the so-called Resistance men of the 'White Army' were common bandits. They had 'taken a dive in the forest' years before, after deserting from the crumbling Belgian Army of 1940, and had lived there ever since, existing on what they could rob, taking bribes from both the Germans and genuine Belgian resisters, terrorising the local farmers and their womenfolk, knowing that with the end of the war their savage, brutal lives would come to an end in front of a firing squad, whoever won.

Now, as Mallory's mind raced and he wondered what he should do next, he told himself that formerly Occupied

Europe had been full of such types who had profited from defeat and subsequent occupation by violence with weapons or from behind a desk, armed with a pen. He knew at that moment, his heart beating more rapidly with tension and suspense, that he would never trust a European of a certain age ever again. The Germans had corrupted them and they had corrupted the Germans. For such folk, patriotism had become a dirty word and would remain thus for ever more. Loot and profit, they had become the leitmotiv of their lives and would remain so. Europe, despite the Nazi boasts of their 'New Order' changing the corrupt, decadent old continent, was just as venial and crooked as it had ever been. It would always be so.

Mallory shook his head impatiently like some beast in the field trying to shake off the flies and dismissed that particularly unpleasant thought.

Five minutes later they were skirting the position where they had heard the unknown soldier whistling the old French marching tune. What was he doing out there? Who was he? Why was he so damned careless, giving his position away just like that . . . ? A myriad questions ran through the Marauders' heads as they marched steadily south-east down that corner of Luxembourg which bulged into Germany. But they remained without answer. It was like so many inexplicable events remembered by the survivors of that war nearly a half a century old now. A mystery that would be never solved: a footnote in the life of men who themselves were unimportant, cannon-fodder at the best, destined to become minor footnotes to World War Two themselves.

But of one thing the Marauders were certain. There were men in the forests everywhere. Sometimes they signalled their presence by a sudden flare. At other times it was the surprised roar of a vehicle engine, being revved mightily in the freezing night air: a sudden column of blacked-out truck headlights glimpsed on a road through the forest. Now and again it was merely a pungent whiff of the coarse black cigarettes which the German soldier smoked or even that typical smell of an unwashed, lice-ridden body; for by now the German Army, that which had once conquered Europe from Cracow to the Channel, was running out of soap.

Just before dawn Mallory was forced at last to allow his Marauders to rest. They were men of iron, picked for their military cunning, but also for their endurance and stamina. But the long night march under impossible conditions had taken its toll. They needed a break. But as tired as he was, Mallory could not settle down into a groggy stupor like the rest. He *had* to know what lay ahead. For there was still a good three-quarters of an hour before first light at this time of the year and by then he wanted his men under real cover where they could lie up for the day before they crossed into Germany and from there advanced into the 'lion's den', as Gavin had called it with a mocking smile, adding, 'if you'll forgive the kids' fairy tale stuff, Commander.' His smile had vanished. 'Because I can tell you here and now this is going to be no teddy bears' picnic. Of that you can be sure.'

After what Gavin had told him then, Mallory knew that it was certainly not going to be any 'teddy bears' picnic'. With his handful of lightly armed men, he had less than a day to break into the POW camp, find the missing general, spirit him halfway across the enemy city of Trier, probably packed with Hun soldiers, and get to the rendezvous.

As he staggered forward at the head of his weary men, Mallory hardly dare think about that 'rendezvous'. That, he knew implicitly, was going to be the toughest patch of the whole 'snatch operation', as Gavin had called it. It was packed with imponderables, not the least the state of the weather on the day of the rescue bid. "God," he said half aloud (like all lonely men in command, Commander Mallory tended to talk to himself), "what a ballsup!"

Another half hour speed march followed. By now it was getting light. Slowly. It was as if some God on high was reluctant to throw light on the miserable war-torn world below. Still, the sky was definitely clearing, though yet again the clouds to the east were heavy with snow, a fact that a weary Mallory didn't know whether he should welcome or not. Snow would make the approach easier, but it did make the final phase of the rescue operation decidedly difficult.

Five minutes later he halted the little column at the edge of the usual fir forest as Thaelmann, in the lead now, held up his hand in warning and called back softly in German (it was Mallory's idea that in any loud conversation they'd use that language as an elementary safety precaution), "*Halt, Leute . . . die Mosel.*"

Mallory caught a glimpse of dull silver between the trees and the steep slopes on either side where the vines grew in the summer and halted the men. "Into the vines," he ordered. Anyone surveying the opposite, Luxembourg bank from the German Hunsruck Mountains on the opposite side of the great border river would spot them in due course, Mallory knew. They had to find some really effective cover to rest and survey the position.

Expertly they crawled forward on their bellies through the snow, leaving no recognisable human tracks, buried themselves in the snow-heavy vines, each one tied up in the traditional eight-branch form so that the sun (when it was there) reflected off the slate which littered the hillside, would reach as many as possible of the budding grapes, and rendezvoused in one of the wooden huts used by the locals for housing their implements.

Mallory let them get their breath for a few minutes, while they huddled, knee to knee, in the tight, smelly interior of what amounted to a toolshed, but glad of the respite from the icy dawn wind, before he said, "Break out your K-rations now. Eat as much as you want. From now on we're going to travel as lightly as possible." He forced a grin, but his single eye didn't light up; he was in no mood for merriment. "I'll make it up for you when we get back for Christmas dinner."

"*If*," Thaelmann said mournfully.

"Shut up," Spiv snapped, "you bloody little ray of German sunshine."

Mallory continued his little briefing. "As soon as we've had a good rest, we'll move forward, looking for somewhere to cross the river to get on the side of the Moselle where the camp is located." He frowned. "We might find a bridge to cross, but I doubt it."

Spiv shivered dramatically. "Personally I don't fancy a dip in the jolly old briny at this time of the sodding year."

Mallory didn't respond. For suddenly he was overcome by the sheer weight of the task ahead and C's final words to him, that day of the doodlebugs in White's: 'The PM wants you and your rogues to go and find him. Alive . . . *or dead.*'

Three

"Down here, dear Sergeant Schulze," *Frau Kreisleiter* Schmeer said in her sexiest little girl voice and bent down to point out the entrance to the bombed-out cellar. She did so slowly and very carelessly to reveal an immense stretch of white thigh surmounted by what looked suspiciously like a fringe of black hairs.

Schulze gulped audibly and murmured, "Christ on a crutch, Matzi, all that meat and no potatoes!" He looked very awed.

"Well, it's sure she's not a true blonde, Schulze, old house – and she's all yours."

Schulze grabbed Matzi's little hand and said fervently, "Don't leave me with her down that cellar, *alter Freund.* Promise me! A man could lose his family jewels down there with a woman like that in zero point nothing seconds."

The little group of troopers pulling the handcart laden with loot for the 'Great Wotan Festive Piss-Up, Ltd', as it was now being called in the Regiment, giggled loudly, but Schulze was too concerned to swing round and berate them, 'make a sow out of them', as he would have done normally.

His old running mate, Matz, was not moved. "Well, you brought it on yersen, you big Bavarian barnshitter," he commented sourly. "Kissing her flipper and bowing an' scraping like a shitting officer and all that stuff. What d'yer expect? You're on yer own, comrade."

"But she's a married women," Schulze said.

"When did that worry you?" Matz responded and set

about clearing away the still smoking rubble from the shattered wine-cellar entrance. To the west of the bombed city, the sirens were beginning to shrill their first warning. Hurriedly the young troopers began to join in, while *Frau* Schmeer said rogueishly, grabbing at Sergeant Schulze's unwilling paw, "Come, my dear Sergeant. I know you are a gallant cavalier of the old school. So I shall trust my honour alone with you in the cellar, once they've finished clearing the entrance." She giggled and rolled her eyes so much that her huge breasts beneath the thin material of her low-cut blouse trembled like puddings.

Schulze held up his hands in mock prayer and intoned piously, "For what we're about to receive, let the Good Lord make us truly grateful." He followed her into the smelly darkness like a sacrificial lamb being led to the slaughter.

Watching, von Dodenburg grinned. His two old rogues were on top form. The prospect of time out of the line, plus a grand slam booze-up always put them in the best of spirits, though he had to admit that Schulze did look slightly apprehensive, for some reason or other.

"Hallo." Someone tapped him on the right shoulder. Automatically his hand flashed to his pistol holster. He caught himself in time. After all he *was* on his home ground, Trier. He turned. It was the girl. "*Morgen, Fraulein Sohmeer*," he said carefully, wishing what had happened hadn't, though it was too late now to worry about such matters.

"*Guten Morgen, Obersturmbannführer*," she responded, looking up at him. Her eyes were hazed and there were deep shadows below them. Still, her youthful cheeks were flushed an apple-red by the December cold and she had that air of youthful, innocent exuberance about her, which was belied by her true character.

"And what brings you down to view the coarse, rough soldiers at their labours this morning?" he asked in what he thought was a light-hearted manner, suitable for a conversation between a hardened soldier pushing thirty and a girl who was barely sixteen.

"You," she whispered. "Will you fuck me again tonight? . . . I need it."

There was no hesitation about her request – and definitely nothing of a sixteen-year-old's innocence. He was shocked. "For God's sake, *Fraulein* Schmeer," he hissed urgently, wondering if the troopers had heard. "Don't talk like that. You could get me sent to Torgau." Von Dodenburg meant the notorious SS prison in the south of Germany.

She laughed cynically. "My dear handsome Kuno—"

Shit on the shingle, he cursed to himself. She knows my first name as well.

"I doubt if you – or I, for that matter – will survive this war." She laughed. It was a hard, brittle sound without the slightest trace of merriment. "Why should we? We don't deserve to, do we?"

"What do you mean—"

His query was interrupted by Schulze's muffled shout from inside the *Weinkeller*. "Sir . . . sir, we've struck liquid gold. Heaps of this stuffing – Hey, d'yer mind, *Frau* Schmeer. I wish yer'd take yer frigging flippers off'n my person . . . I'm not used to that kind of carry-on!"

"Well, you said *stuffing*, Sergeant Schulze," Matz commented with a coarse laugh and then, to the troopers who were crowding forward to look at whatever Sergeant Schulze had discovered, he snapped, businesslike now, "Remember, if it's the real hard stuff, corporals get the first choice." He doubled his little fist, his wizened face threatening. "Otherwise some of you Christmas tree soldiers are going to lose a set of front choppers."

"*Fraulein* Schmeer," von Dodenburg said, forgetting the men in the cellar," the Anglo-American air gangsters will be back soon. Let me take you inside where you'll be safe."

She responded eagerly with, "Yes, inside. We'll use

my parents' bed. The old bastard's up on the hill at the Ami camp and you know where that fat pig my mother is – trying to get the trousers off that big sergeant – Schulze."

'Not much different from her daughter,' von Dodenburg was tempted to say, but then thought better of it. The girl was just on the brink of a nervous breakdown, he could see that. It took only the slightest incident and she would flip. He didn't want that. So he humoured her. "We'll see about that," he said and took her by the arm gently but firmly. "Come on, let's get in the house before the bastards get started."

Up in the *Durchgangslager* on the hill above Trier, *Kreisleiter* Schmeer had already experienced a couple of surprises, too, in his (as he had thought) routine pre-Christmas Eve conference with the middle-aged Camp Commandant. Outside in the dreary surroundings of the POW camp, those Kriegies capable were trawling the usual circuit and the usual half-starved Red Army prisoners were begging for food from the 'rich' Americans or fighting over the cookhouse's pitifully empty swill-bins. It was another day at war like the so many hundred days of war that had preceded this 23rd December 1944. Schmeer, still peeved that his fat wife had not yet satisfied his sexual desires, as modest as they were, even though there were only twenty-four hours left to Christmas, had anticipated the normally boring discussion on how to the feed the Amis and how to transport them to Limburg on the Rhine when the order was given to evacuate them, probably on Christmas Day itself.

But he had been in for a surprise right from the start. The nervous Camp Commandant, whose prime aim at this stage of the war (as it was all too obvious to a devoted coward like Schmeer himself) was to save his own precious hide, had commenced with the statement: "*Kreisleiter*, the prisoners are restless, especially at this time of the year. Apparently they celebrate Christmas in America, too."

The news had startled the Party official and he had blurted out, "I've only got a handful of SS under my command. I'll need those close to Party HQ for security purposes." He meant to protect him. "What are you going to do, *Herr Major*?"

The Camp Commandant had looked at him quite calmly and announced like a man who had everything under total control. "Do not worry about the matter, *Kreisleiter*. I've got everything well in hand. On the morning of Christmas Eve I shall release extra rations to the Ami swine – from their own Red Cross parcels of course, that goes without saying. Then perhaps you'll oblige me with a *fuder** of wine, nothing special, just cheap gutrot. I shall release that mid afternoon; by evening they'll be blind drink. My informant in the camp tells me the Amis have no head for wine. They'll drink it like water."

"Yes, of course, I'll get the wine to you. I know where there's plenty of that sugar-water *Liebfraumilch*, which the Tommies used to like before the war." He shivered dramatically. "But how they could drink that gnat's piss, I'll never know . . . But this informant?" He changed his approach, voice suddenly cagey. "Who?"

The Camp Commandant tugged the end of his long nose thoughtfully. Obviously he was enjoying being the centre of attention for once. "I'd rather not say at this stage, *Kreisleiter*, because—"

"Because?" the fat official urged.

The CO lowered his voice and glanced at the steamed-up windows, as if he half expected someone to be listening there. "As you know, the Gestapo are to come here—"

Schmeer waved for him to get on with it impatiently. "Yes, I know . . . Your informant?"

"Perhaps, *Kreisleiter*, if there is a sudden emergency, my informant could ensure that we are moved from here to Mainz before the real trouble starts."

* *Fuder* is a thousand litre barrel of wine.

"We . . . trouble?" *Kreisleiter* Schmeer stuttered, completely lost now. "I don't understand."

The CO smiled at him, as if he were suddenly confronted by a simpleton. "Naturally in an emergency your SS would be needed up here. You – and I for that matter – would be in real danger."

"Yes," Schmeer quavered, fat jowls trembling mightily at the thought.

"So, if we could take off before everything gets out of hand, and my informant is my early warning system in a way, we'd be out from under by the time the balloon really goes up."

"But what kind of excuse would you find to take yourself – and me, naturally too – off to Mainz and abandon the camp to what is to come? You know the Führer's secret order that the couple of hundred thousand Allied POWs in our camps are going to be the ultimate blackmail. At five minutes to twelve," – Schmeer used the German expression for 'the eleventh hour' – "We start shooting them in batches of a thousand at a time. That should settle the Allies' hash for them."

"Yes . . . yes," the Camp Commandant agreed urgently. "But the Führer in his infinite wisdom has forgotten that there will be few camp commandants who will risk being strung up by the neck for shooting Allied POWs in the provinces when our dearly beloved Leader" – he lowered his head momentarily in reverence – "is so far away in Berlin. No, my dear *Kreisleiter* Schmeer, nowadays it's everyone for himself and the devil help the hindmost." He paused for breath and continued, "So you ask what kind of pawn have I got in my hands which would warrant an emergency recall to Mainz?"

Outside the Russians were rioting again. One of the middle-aged guards' dogs had slipped its leash and got into the camp. It had been its last move. For the half-starved wretches, the 'Ivans' as the Germans called them, had brought the beast down, throttled it and were now skinning it with sharpened can lids – or were attempting to do so. For already fighting had broken out between them for the prized liver, filled with life-giving vitamins and so soft that it could be eaten raw. The Camp Commandant shrugged. He had seen it all before. In a few moments the guards would fire a volley over the Ivans' heads to disperse them, or if they were in a bad mood at being disturbed, they'd fire directly at the Russian prisoners. One way or other, the Commandant told himself, it didn't matter. The Russians wouldn't survive the war. Even if they did, that crazy dictator of theirs, Stalin, would have them shot once they had crossed the border back into the 'Soviet Paradise'; they'd surrendered, hadn't they?

The CO answered his rhetorical question. "Hardly a pawn really, more like a bishop, *Kreisleiter*."

"Holy strawsack, get on with it, Major."

"A general," he said hastily, not liking Schmeer's tone one bit. But still he needed him – for a while yet. "Somewhere in my little camp I have a full-blown American general."

"You mean, Sturz wasn't—" Schmeer caught himself in time before he blurted out what the four-eyed masturbator had told him. One way that he had survived here in Trier over the years was that he had kept his mouth shut on important matters; played one person off against another. Let the Major think he held all the trumps, for the time being. Who knew when Sturz could be used to be played against the Camp Commandant? So he held his peace and asked innocently, "I suppose you and Captain Sturz will know all about him?"

"Sturz knows nothing. Frankly, *Kreisleiter*, I don't trust Sturz one little bit. After all, we all know that he is a one hundred and seventy-fiver, don't we?" He lowered his voice at the dreaded name, one given to homosexuals, after the paragraph – 175 – in the German Legal Code dealing with unnatural sex.

"Of course . . . of course," Schmeer agreed hastily.

The Camp Commandant smiled winningly at him. "It will all be taken care of in due course, *Kreisleiter*. Out there, my dear fellow, is our passport to the future, whatever happens in the next weeks." He raised his voice, obviously feeling in complete charge of the situation. "Now I suggest we relax. After all, the day is young and the morrow is the blessed feast of Christmas." He pressed the bell on his desk, still beaming at Schmeer, whose brain was racing frantically, trying to assess all the new possibilities and how they would affect him.

As if she had been standing behind the door, waiting for the Camp Commandant's summons, a girl appeared, followed by another, with a napkin over her arm and bearing a tray with bottles and champagne glasses on it. "A *piccolo* of champus each, my dear fellow," the CO said expansively, "or more than one if you so desire."

Schmeer didn't respond for a moment. Instead he stared at the two girls, both in their early twenties. He hadn't seen girls like that in Trier since 1938 when he'd help to burn the synagogue down. Naturally the Roman legacy had left many women on the Moselle with dark Latin looks and flashing black eyes that didn't fit in at all with the creed of Aryan purity that the Party propagated. But these were not Latins; there was that something a little extra, a little '*rassig*'. "My God," he exclaimed, as the first one spoke in perfect German, fluttering her eyelashes at him in a decidedly provocative manner, "they're Jewesses."

The Camp Commandant chuckled with delight at his surprise. "*Natürlich, mein lieber Schmeer*," he exclaimed. "There's no mistaking them, and look at the breasts on the second one – what a pair of melons!" He restrained himself with difficulty. "A bit different from our decent, but homely local girls, what?"

"But Jewish women – *here*?!"

The Camp Commandant laughed. "You'd be surprised, *Kreisleiter*, at just how useful Jews can be even in a place like this." His voice was businesslike again. He addressed the first one, snapping, "All right, Sarah, don't just stand there. Serve the bubbly and then let's get down to business." He started tugging at the belt of his breeches, fat face suddenly red.

Four

Somewhere an owl hooted. Over the River Moselle a low mist hung, deadening every other sound, save the soft lap-lap of the water at the foot of the high bank. Over on the other side there would be sentries patrolling the towpath next to the medieval toll-house. But they could not hear them. It was a perfect night for what they had in mind.

Behind Mallory, crouched there in the freezing mist, alert for the first sign of danger, Spiv and Kitchener were tying hessian strips about the rowlocks of the little boat they had stolen from the boathouse further up the bank. Around them the others crouched, hessian sacks slung over their shoulders to hide their uniforms, their caps stuffed in their pockets. They'd only reveal that they were Allied soldiers if things got desperate.

Not that the one-eyed commander feared they'd be disturbed on the western bank this night. The fog and the Allied raid had cleared the whole area as if a great hand had swept the Moselle flood plain and magicked everyone away. They might well have been the last people alive on the earth. He took one last look. Nothing! He wiped the wet mistdrops from his tense face and whistled softly. It was the signal.

One by one they got into the ramshackle little boat, while Mallory, the only experienced sailor among them, held the boat close to the shore to prevent it from rocking excessively. Fortunately the fog was thickening and pretty well muffled any sound they made. All the same, Mallory told himself, anyone coming down the towpath couldn't fail to hear the clumsy efforts of his Marauders to get into the boat. Finally it was done. He took his place at the rudder, knowing as he did so that their crossing of the Moselle was going to be pretty much hit-or-miss. The fog was too dense now for him to steer to the opposite bank with any degree of accuracy. "All right, Spiv," he whispered. "You too, Peters."

His two oarsmen whispered back their agreement. He gave the overladen craft a push and they were off. Somewhere there was the muffled sound of one of Trier's many churches striking midnight. It was the witching hour, Mallory thought. By the time they were across, the sentries would have been changed by the guard commander and they would have settled into the boring four-hour spell in front of them, trying to keep their eyes open and their bodies from freezing with the night cold. No wonder the infantrymen called this the 'graveyard shift'.

Time passed leadenly. The muffled sound of the oars, the occasional splash of water from the oarblades, the steady breathing of the oarsmen, seemed to have a soporific effect. As cold as it was on the water, Mallory fought off the urge to close his one eye. He swore he could have fallen asleep there and then if he had allowed himself to do so. Perhaps it was tension. He didn't know. All he knew was he had to ensure that he kept with the current, which he already knew flowed at an angle from west to east. If he missed it, he could be swept all the way to Thionville in France. Once they got into the gorges downstream, the quickening rush of water wouldn't have given them much of a chance to gain the bank.

Up front, good, loyal Peters gave as much help as he could, relaying his information back through Kitchener, who passed it on to Mallory. Not that there was much that Peters could see. One time he had ordered a halt; he had feared he had heard an engine in the distance. But it had turned out to be the cry of some nightbird, and after a few heart-stopping moments they had moved on again, hoping against hope that they were heading in the right direction. If they weren't . . . Mallory shrugged a little helplessly at the thought. If dawn caught them on the open river. He preferred not to think that unpleasant prospect through to an end. They moved on.

By the time it had grown dark and the blackouts had been put up personally by the Camp Commandant and his two 'personal assistants', as he called them, *Kreisleiter* Schmeer was, as he would have put it, 'piss blue and as sharp as a howitzer' – in other words, sozzled and sex-crazy. He could barely keep his hands off the lush charms of the two 'assistants'. Jewish or not, he told himself, head full of drunken fantasies, they were women – *available women*. That was for sure. For by the time the blackouts had been put up and the door locked, with a red handkerchief thrown over the single light to give the bare room a warm red glow, the Camp Commandant had his breeches off and was allowing himself to be fondled by the taller of the two women, who called him 'my little cheetah', as if she really meant it.

It took Schmeer some time to overcome his own inhibitions. They were Jewesses and he was an important official in the Party. In reality he was worried whether he could perform in that company, where he was definitely the oldest. A bottle of two of bubbly later, helped by copious chasers of Korn, the strong local gin, and he had cast all such inhibitions to one side.

The girls relaxed more, too. *They* were in control now and obviously they liked being so. Giggling hysterically, the taller of the two, Heidi, dipped a befuddled Schmeer's middle finger into a glass of champagne and staring at the magnified image in the glass, she declared that would be the size of Schmeer's sexual organ. That pleased the drunken, purple-faced *Kreisleiter* no end and he did not object when Heidi and Karen, the other Jewess, had pulled off his boots and breeches, he nearly falling over drunkenly in the process, to reveal his naked lower body.

Nothing!

Schmeer stared down at his flaccid worm and felt it was no use. The girls thought to the contrary. Cheered on by the Camp Commandant, who now, for some reason, was wearing Heidi's red, art-silk knickers on the top of his balding head and waving an empty champagne bottle wildly, the two women, clad only in girdle and black stockings, danced together obscenely (Schmeer thought it might have been a tango – not that it mattered), holding each other tight and cheek to cheek until a pop-eyed Schmeer started to feel the first faint stirrings of lust in his loins.

Hastily he flashed a look at his groin. Yes, there was no mistaking it. There was definite, if slight, movement down there! "More," he cried joyously. "*More, please.*" He started to laugh uncontrollably.

Now the room started to revolve around Schmeer. The hysterical giggling of the girls and the thick, heavy grunting of the Camp Commandant, who had now mounted Karen from behind, grew and receded like the ebb and flow of the tide. The room grew ever redder. Vaguely Schmeer was aware of wet hot lips nuzzling his groin. He felt happy . . . happier than he had felt for years. "If this is the end," he murmured thickly, apropos of nothing, "give me defeat . . ." The red tide came over closer. He tried to fight it back. Impossible. He could no longer feel the hot wetness between his legs. Then suddenly, almost startlingly, he was gone. The red tide submerged him.

Sergeant Rosenstein peered through the crack in the window beyond the ill-fitting blackout and told himself, as he surveyed the two drunken and now unconscious Kraut slobs, that the girls had done their work well – too well. For an idle moment, he wondered how they could stand being dicked by the same Krauts who had sent them to camps in the first place. Then he dismissed the thought as irrelevant. They were '*sabras*' born in Palestine, smuggled into the camps like he had been, to survive first and then to organise. They had done their duty, like he was doing, as good soldiers should, working for the future of a new nation yet to be created.

Despite the biting night cold, Sergeant Rosenstein felt a flush of proud warmth surge through his tough body. With girls like that from good Jewish families how could they fail? But as yet there were many problems facing them – they had to have people, and in a terrible way, the Nazis had done the emerging state a favour by collecting all of Europe's Jews in these death camps. They, toughened and hardened by their experiences, would be the volunteers for the Israel to come. Everyone's hand was against them. So they needed every possible weapon, however terrible, to get those people, *who had to survive*, to the Promised Land. He raised the camera (it was the camp's own for photographing every new prisoner for the *Durchgangslager* files). He knocked carefully on the window-pane.

The two nearly naked girls knew what to do – they had been well briefed. They posed lecherously, licking their lips with professional concupiscence, thrusting out their bellies, adorned by that hairy triangle of dark black, while behind them the drunken Party official and the Camp Commandant sprawled naked, out to the world, snoring loudly. Sergeant Rosenfield allowed himself a grin and then he pressed the shutter. A flash of icy white blinding light. He had his shot: all he'd need now for the blackmail to come. Hastily Sergeant Rosenstein disappeared into the night. Behind him the two girls began sorting things out, putting on their clothes, hiding the precious black-market currency – cigarettes – inside their blouses, busy with stealing whatever they could. It was two o'clock in the morning of Christmas Eve . . .

A mile or so away, Mallory and his Marauders were approaching the other bank now. The mist over the river was beginning to thin. Now and again, an anxious Mallory, steering, could glimpse the opposite bank and note thankfully that it appeared empty save for foxholes here and there, newly dug to judge from the fresh brown earth against the background of frozen white.

Up front the others kept a tense lookout, while Spiv and his fellow Marauder, breathing hard, propelled the boat ever closer to the bank. Now none of them had time for the usual banter that usually accompanied their ops. The situation was too dangerous. At any moment the challenge could ring out '*Wer da?*' – to be followed an instant later by an angry hiss of machine gun fire which would mean the end. Now each man was preoccupied by his own thoughts, wrapped up in a tight cocoon of fear and apprehension. Never had the Marauders been in a situation as fraught with danger as this.

When, however, the alarm was sounded, it caught the men in the boat completely by surprise. For it came, not to the front, but to the rear, from the mid-stream of the Moselle, to be exact, the old pre-war shipping channel.

Suddenly, startlingly, a cold beam of silver light cut through the gloom. "*Duck*!" Mallory hissed urgently. Now he could hear the muffled chug-chug of a motor boat on the river, cruising at low speed. The icy finger parted the fog. It grew closer. Now all of them could hear the boat coming closer. Had its occupants heard them? They hardly dared breathe as they lay and crouched there in a muddled heap, hearts beating furiously, their whole beings focused on that light which came steadily closer.

"It's going to get us," Peters hissed.

Mallory knew he was right. They hadn't a chance in hell of avoiding that light. The occupants of the boat would possibly think that their rowing boat had been cut adrift from the other bank, perhaps by shellfire or the bombs earlier that night. All the same, they could well come closer just to drag in the drifting craft to their own side of the bank. Any sensible military authority would do so, especially when they were facing the prospect of an enemy making an assault crossing of the

Moselle sooner or later. They'd ensure that nothing was left behind for the attackers to use. Slowly, very slowly, Mallory started to draw the big Colt automatic from its holster underneath the smelly hessian sacking which he had used to drape his upper body. He'd hate like hell to use it, but it seemed at that moment that it was going to be the only way out: a swift slug into the light and then over the side, swimming like hell for the opposite bank.

Thaelmann beat him to it. To the surprise of the others he raised himself and balancing awkwardly, cupped his hands around his mouth: "*Sie da*," he shouted in his native tongue. "*Hey Sie!*"

Instantly the light flashed in his direction. In a second he was outlined, shielding his eyes against the glare, in a circle of silver light. "*Was machen Sie da?*" a harsh voice, distorted metallically by a megaphone, demanded.

"*Volkssturm*," Thaelmann answered. "*Kompanie Porta Nigra*." He meant the Home Guard stationed around the famous Roman monument 'the Black Gate' (Porta Nigra). "*Wir haben den Auftrag all Boote am andern Ufer zu sammeln*."

"*Um diese Uhrzeit*!" the man with megaphone cried a little surprised. "At this time?"

"*Wann sonst*?" Thaelmann answered steadfastly, not a tremor of uncertainty in his voice. "No Ami'll bother us at this time of the night. They'll all be tucked up in their little bunks playing with the old five-fingered widow." He laughed coarsely.

His laugh was answered. Suddenly the light clicked off, leaving them blinking in the sudden inky darkness. "On your way, comrade, before dawn," the unknown speaker warned. "Expect another Ami raid then. *Mach's gut*."

"*Danke*," Thaelmann answered and sat down abruptly as the boat chugged away.

At the oars, Kitchener said thickly, "I'm feeling I am going to urinate myself."

"*Feeling*," Spiv snorted. "I pissed mesen a minute ago."

The others laughed weakly. Then they were on their way again. The last hurdle had about been cleared. It was six hours now till dawn on Christmas Eve, 1944.

Five

"Look at the conniving bastard," 'Green Smoke' the Texan said bitterly, as he peered through the slit in the canvas screening of the crapper. He groaned. He was suffering from the squitter's again, as they all were. Outside, the frozen snow was splashed red with the blood of the afflicted Kriegies and here and there were bundled stained underpants of those who had not been able to reach the privy in time. "Typical moxie two-timer. Why he's even bringing in broads for the Krauts now. Pimp bastard!"

Horowitz peeped through the slit opposite where he squatted, too, straining and fighting the stabbing pain in his churning guts. Sergeant Rosenstein was escorting two women in high heels across the parade ground, holding their hands on the slippery frozen bits like some medieval gallant as they headed for the waiting truck, its exhaust gas fogging the freezing dawn air. He frowned. Rosenstein certainly was pushing his luck in front of the other American POWs. What the hell was he doing parading the women in this way?

"I . . . I . . . wouldn't trust the bastard," Green Smoke forced out the words with a grimace, as his innards flowed from him once more in a sudden burst, "as far as I could throw him – which ain't far, buddy. But one day—" He stopped in mid-word and let his bowels run in a gush once more. "Christ, I swear I lost my ring that time." His face glistened with sweat in the semi-darkness of the latrine and Horowitz felt for him. Most of those who were suffering from the squitters daren't leave the crapper any more. In the huts the piss-buckets were full to overflowing and those who weren't sick had no desire to have their packed quarters polluted by the nauseating stench of 'green smoke', as the Texan called his illness. The sick had to stay outside in the freezing cold of the dawn parade ground or in the evil-smelling, stomach-churning privy.

Horowitz watched as Rosenstein helped the girls into the back of the truck. Both revealed ample lengths of shapely black-clad legs, but there were no wolf-whistles forthcoming from the men in the privy; they simply hadn't the strength. That task completed, Rosenstein handed something to the middle-aged '*landser*' slumped on the tailgate and slapped the canvas to inform the driver he could leave.

"The bribe from that Kraut bastard, the Commandant," Green Smoke said. "Probably stolen from one of our Red Cross – and that guy Rosenstein is supposed to represent our interests." He moaned and added, "Man-of-confidence . . . *my aching arse!*"

Horowitz waited till the tall, ashen-faced Texan had recovered a little before asking with apparent casualness, "Were you here when he first arrived?"

"Sure. I got taken with the Eighth Div, in the Hurtgen Forest in November. He came in a little later. Funny." He frowned thoughtfully. "He wore the div patch – you know, the golden eight – and when some of the guys asked him about his outfit, he didn't seem to answer and he came in the next day wearing the 'bloody bucket' patch." The sick Texan meant the red bucket patch of the US 28th Division. "We was all too fucked up at the time to think about it much, but now . . ." He shrugged and wished he hadn't, because the movement must have affected his poor stomach and he was seized by yet another agonised spasm. Once more the latrine was filled with the stomach of 'green smoke' as the Texan evacuated his diseased bowels for the umpteenth time. Horowitz decided he'd had enough. The stink was impossible. He'd take a chance on his own guts and hope he'd be able to make the privy before he got caught short. "See you, buddy," he said, buckling up his pants.

"Yeah," the big Texan commented, still racked by pain,

"if I ain't wasted away. Hell, you'll know where to find—" His words ended in a groan, followed by the fast flow of liquid. Hurriedly, Horowitz, gagging as he did so, left.

A little at a loss, Horowitz limped about the camp. The mist had cleared. He guessed it was going to be a freezingly cold day, but fine. Already he could see the contrails left by the last of the RAF bombers, heading home after a night's work of destruction for their bases in Yorkshire and East Anglia for a breakfast of bacon and egg and real coffee. "Lucky jerks," he said enviously to no one in particular. For at this time of the day before the morning *appell*, there was never anybody about, save for the odd Kraut 'ferret' in his blue overalls carrying his metal rod for prodding under the raised huts to check for escape tunnels. Not that there'd be any. The men were too dispirited and the earth was ice-hard anyway.

He limped in the direction of the kitchen. He might be able to panhandle a cup of weak peppermint tea from the guys detailed to fetch 'breakfast' for the Kriegies, which they ate on the same bunks they'd slept in. The 'tea' bore no resemblance to any tea he'd ever drunk before, but it was wet and hot at least.

"Mo." The urgent whisper caught him by surprise. He didn't know any one in the POW camp who knew his first name. He swung round, startled. It was Rosenstein. He was lounging against the wall. In one hand he had a big *wurst* sandwich; in the other one a canteen cup of steaming hot coffee – and by the fragrance coming from it, Horowitz guessed that it was made of 'real bean' coffee. His stomach did a quick flip-flop at that delightful odour.

Rosenstein saw the look on the General's face and said easily, offering him the metal cup, "Here, take the java. There's plenty more where that came from, sir."

Horowitz took the cup gratefully. It seemed an age since he had last drunk a cup of decent American coffee. But the ease with which Rosenstein proffered this precious gift added to his suspicion of the man. He seemed to have everything and be able to do virtually anything in the camp. Naturally Horowitz knew that the NCO was 'a big man in the company office'. But that didn't explain everything. What about the women, probably whores, whom he had just seen off? Who had allowed him to bring them into the camp and, more importantly, why had he been able to see them off to God knows where so blatantly in broad daylight? There was more to Sergeant Rosenstein, who had been able to change his divisional patches without any apparent problems, that met the eye.

But before Horowitz could ask any questions, Sergeant Rosenstein lowered his voice and said in a conspiratorial fashion, "We go tonight."

"Go?" he asked, astonished.

"Yeah, out of here. They'll all be bombed by then, guards and prisoners. Then we blow."

"But how?"

"You saw the truck with the – er – ladies, didn't ya? Well it's coming again tonight. The Commandant still wants to get his ashes hauled." Rosenstein grinned, his face cynical and all-knowing. "So we bring in the dames again for him. But tonight the truck will depart a little earlier and then it's gonna be Happy Christmas for you and me."

"But—" Horowitz began to protest.

Rosenstein didn't give him a chance. "Take yer time with the java. If you want a refill, ask the hash-slinger inside." He jerked his thumb in the direction of the cookhouse. "Tell him I sent you. It'll be okay." He touched his garrison cap casually. "See ya on the outside, General. Perhaps you can get me a three-day pass to Pig Ally." He meant Paris' Place Pigalle. And with that he sauntered off, as if he didn't have a care in the world, leaving Horowitz to stare at his broad well-fed frame in complete astonishment.

Von Dodenburg shook his head. It hurt and he wished

he hadn't. The room came into focus. His vision was still, however, blurred. He shook his head once more. Now everything came into view.

Slowly he let his gaze wander round the room. Her clothes were everywhere, tossed about the bedroom carelessly, as if she had been in a very great haste to get them off, which he now recalled she had. Her white schoolkid's pants were screwed into a tight ball and thrown on to a chair. Her sweater was spread-eagled over the end of the bed like a headless swimmer. She didn't have a bra; her breasts weren't big enough. That reminded him. He swallowed hard, thinking of his guilt once more.

He turned, still naked, flesh goose-bumped in the morning cold. Schmeer's daughter, that 'German Maiden', who was definitely no 'maiden', von Dodenburg mused, was still asleep. She lay face down in the rumpled bed, snoring slightly, the down *federdecke* thrown back to reveal her naked body, her slim legs still spread to reveal the pubic puff.

Von Dodenburg frowned. He had got to stop this business. He was a regimental commander, now responsible for the lives of 200 young men. He should be able to control himself.

The girl groaned. Her eyes opened momentarily, closed again and then opened once more. "Kiss me," she said hoarsely and opened her arms.

He did so perfunctorily.

She swept back the long tress of blond hair from her unlined forehead and looked up at him, quite seriously for her. "What's wrong?" she asked.

"This!" He indicated the bed.

"Why?"

He shrugged his broad shoulders, both scarred with livid weals from a fight with a Ivan Cossack back in 1943. "It's wrong. It's nice," he added hastily, "but wrong. I shouldn't be doing this—"

"Do you think you were the first?" she interrupted, grinning a little, making him feel like a tongue-tied schoolboy in the presence of some experienced 'pavement pounder'.

"No, of course not. But your age . . . your father."

"My father," she sneered. Reaching out, she took one of his cigarettes without asking, lit it and puffed out a twin stream of blue smoke – and the cynical comment, "Our Führer says a good German girl doesn't smoke or use make-up. My father – that pious hypocrite! All he thinks about is filling his pockets, saving his fat hide and, if he can, sticking it in some poor woman who's scared to death that he'll send her to one of the camps if she doesn't touch his dirty little thing." Her breasts heaved delightfully, the little pink nipples erect with the cold of the bedroom.

He looked down at her, as shocked as he ever could be these days. "How can you say such things?"

She laughed hollowly. "Where have you been the last two or three years?" she countered.

"At the front."

"I'm sure the air's cleaner there," she said. "But here in the Homeland, everyone is out for himself. Times have changed. Now we're nearing the end, we might as well enjoy what we have, don't you think?" She smiled up at him through half-closed eyes and opened her skinny schoolgirl's legs slowly and seductively. Now he could see her full nakedness. The hairy fringe around the pale pink slit the last source of real pleasure in this crazy war-torn, doomed world, he told himself as he inclined forward to her.

"You see," she whispered, looking down at his naked stomach. "An erection at least doesn't have a conscience."

He said nothing. He felt his heart start to pound once more although he knew what she wanted – and he too, he had to admit – was wrong. Youth, German Youth, ought not to be so cynical, to give up so easily. What had the Führer once said about Germany's young people? They had to be as 'tough as leather, as hard as Krupp steel and as speedy as a greyhound'. What would he say to these amoral, cynical, defeatist kids?

"Come on," she whispened huskily, running her cunning little pink tongue around her red, wet lips seductively, "you know you want it. Push it into me. I'd just faint if you did." Her grip on his upper arms tightened almost cruelly. "Give it to me. Be a swine. Make me scream. Torture me." Her pale face was flushing red. Tiny beads of sweat were gathering at her hairline. He breathing was becoming shallow and fast. She raised her stomach to meet his. "Oh, don't wait anymore. Slide it – all of it—"

"*HAPPY FRIGGING CHRISTMAS!*" That well-known, tremendous voice shattered the morning stillness. "*HAPPY FRIGGING CHRISTMAS TO YOU ALL, SOLDIERS* . . . And a piss-poor bunch o' wet-tails you are."

"*FROHES FEST, OBERSCHARFUHRER*!" came back the deep bass answer from a couple of hundred young throats.

Von Dodenburg felt his erection disappear as swiftly as it had appeared. "I must go and urinate," he said hastily, raising himself from the bed.

"No, no," she whined, like a spoiled child denied some special delicacy. "I've got to have it *now*!"

Von Dodenburg ignored her pleading. Instead he started to slip into his uniform, glad that Schulze had disturbed him from what he had intended. Already he was feeling better that he had not gone ahead with what the now pouting girl had wanted so desperately.

"Now this is the drill, you bunch o' warm brothers," Schulze was saying, as, half-dressed, von Dodenburg hurried by *Kreisleiter* Schmeer, his head wrapped in a vinegar-soaked bandage for some reason known to himself as he sat there next to the kitchen oven groaning softly and rocking back and forth, as if he was in some pain, "and if yer don't get it shitting right, I'll have the Vaseline to your asses, Christmas Eve or no shitting Christmas Eve . . . Corporal Matz, give them the afternoon's schedule."

"All right, pin back yer spoons," Matz took up the briefing. "All work ceases at thirteen hundred hours precisely.

There'll be nigger sweat and cake – courtesy of *Frau Kreisleiter* Schmeer." Even as he directed a steaming jet of liquid at the centre of the toilet bowl, von Dodenburg could detect the special note in the little Corporal's voice at the mention of the District Leader's fat wife. He grinned despite his headache. "Plus a bottle of beer, real Munich suds, for those of you greenbeaks who are old enough to sup suds."

"Get on with it, Corporal," Schulze intoned, all senior sergeant now. "I don't want you piss-arsed junior noncoms wasting my valuable time."

As he dried himself, von Dodenburg thought he heard Matz mutter a rude suggestion about what Sergeant Schulze might do with his time, but he concluded that would be an anatomical impossibility.

"At fifteen hundred hours precisely," Matz boomed, "we congregate in the school hall. Everyone in his best uniform, badges and buttons polished. Hair combed and for those of yer who shave, get the frigging fluff off'n yer ugly mugs . . ."

While Corporal Matz took care of the Christmas Eve festivities, Sergeant Schulze set off to enjoy his own private pre-Xmas feast and as he would undoubtedly have said himself, 'Brother, I don't mean stuffing a frigging goose!' For the big NCO, with a face that looked as if it had been chiselled out of red brick with a blunt instrument, had more on his mind than just fodder and suds this Christmas of 1944. As he told himself in eager anticipation, grabbing at the front of his bulging trousers, as if to reassure himself that his piece of first-class German salami was still there, there's more to Christmas than filling yer guts. There certainly was; for Sergeant Schulze had concluded that the sad state of affairs which was currently causing him to limp badly was a direct result of unrequited love.

He knew it was wrong. She wasn't for him. Matz had told him so. "Heaven, arse and cloudburst," the little Corporal had exclaimed when he had disclosed to his old comrade what his own pre-Christmas present was going to be, "get yersen in between those tits with yer ugly mug and yer ears'll jam so much, that yer'll never get out agen – *alive!*"

"I know . . . . I know," he had retorted wildly. "but I can't help myself. I'm in love . . . I must have her – *or die*!"

As melodramatic as that statement was, Sergeant Schulze did not know when he uttered it that Christmas Eve morning that it was far closer to the truth than he could ever have imagined. Thus he hurried away, bowed with the weight of a slight erection already, bound for his date with destiny.

The stage was set, the actors were in place, the drama could commence . . .

PART FOUR

Black Xmas

"Happy landings, Joe . . . If anyone can make it, kid, you can!" General Gavin yelled above the roar of the C-47, its pilot trying out his twin engines at full throttle, filling the dawn air with the cloying stench of aviation fuel.

It was barely after dawn, but on the makeshift airfield just outside 1st Army HQ at Châteaufontaine all was hectic activity. Trucks roared down the main highway with their lights burning despite the blackout regulations. Crew chiefs and loaders ran back and forth with their checkboards, yelling red-faced orders, cursing the men from the 'Red Ball Express'. Staff officers looked worried. Noncoms blew urgent blasts on their whistles. Local Belgian workers shuffled back and forth in their sabots, pocketing nearly anything that fell from the crates that were piled everywhere, for sale on the Liège black market. All was controlled chaos. Bastogne – held by the US 101st Airborne Division and surrounded by the Germans – was going to be re-supplied again this morning before the snow came, and the armada was eager to be off.

Gavin was too. But in his case he wasn't worried about the trapped fellow paras. His concern was the glider to be piloted by Major Joe Gansenheimer, who wore a casual leather jacket, sunglasses (for what reason Gavin couldn't fathom in view of the fact that it was late December); and his blond hair far too long for a major. He smiled faintly. Major Joe Gansenheimer, veteran of Normandy, Holland, and the recent glider-landing in Bastogne, looked all of eighteen years old. He could well have been Gavin's own son, if he'd had one.

Still, Gansenheimer was typical of the airborne pilots, young, cocky, unconventional, just the right sort of guy for the tough, unorthodox mission that lay ahead of him. He cupped his hands around his mouth, the prop wash from the C-47 whipping his elegant uniform tightly around his lean body. "Joe," he yelled to the pilot, "it's not going to be easy. You could well buy a farm."

Gansenheimer laughed easily at the prospect of 'buying the farm' – dying – and yelled back, "It's gonna be a piece o' cake, General."

Gavin nodded. "'Kay, this is the latest poop from Corps HQ, Joe. You're going to get the most support we can give you without giving the game away. You'll be escorted by three P-51s" – he meant Mustang fighters – "till you reach the Moselle. They'll see off any unwelcome Kraut visitors."

Gansenheimer nodded his understanding. Up ahead, the towplane had cut back its engines. The crew chief and his team were making last minute adjustments to the rope that held the two planes together. Gansenheimer flexed his powerful biceps. Take-off was always one hell of a strain on the arms. The prop wash and turbulence was sometimes so bad that it needed two men to hold the controls. This time he'd have to do it alone; there was no one else in the Waco glider.

"In addition," Gavin went on, "Eighth Air Force in the UK has signalled they're bringing their planned attack on the area forward by an hour to accommodate us."

"Bully for the Eighth Air Force," Gansenheimer commented with a cheeky youthful grin on his plump-cheeked, freckled face, so that he looked like something drawn by Norman Rockwell for the front cover of the *Saturday Evening Post*.

Gavin shared his grin momentarily, but for no longer. The situation was too serious for any fooling around, including tough wisecracks. Leave that kind of crap, the General told himself, to John Wayne in a Hollywood war movie. That was Tinseltown style. This was war where people got killed – *dead*. "They're gonna plaster targets all along the general Moselle area from Saarburg to the south of the city – Trier – to Wittlich in the North. With a bit of luck, the sirens will send everyone to the shelters in Trier and you'll be able to slip in unnoticed."

"Famous last words," the boyish pilot cracked, a smile on his broad face, as he made a few last minute adjustments to his primitive controls. He saw the worried look on Gavin's features and added swiftly, "Anyway, General, most of the locals ought to be stinko by then. I know I would be if I were off duty."

Gavin smiled at the boy. For all he knew, a glass of 3.5 wartime beer would put him out under the table in any saloon. The kid was probably a virgin still. A lot of 'em died before they ever lost their cherry.

Up on the slight rise, an officer was raising his Very pistol to fire the signal for the first plane to take off to Bastogne. Gavin nodded his approval. If the Krauts were monitoring the American Air Corps traffic this morning – and they probably were – they'd follow the first flights and soon calculate that the air armada was heading for Bastogne. Thereafter they'd be too busy to notice the lone plane slipping away from the rest and heading due east. Well, Gavin hoped so, at least.

"Here we go, General!" Gansenheimer roared, as the green flare shot into the sky and exploded. It hung there, colouring all the suddenly upturned faces a sickly unnatural hue.

Gavin stepped back. Gansenheimer waved, pushed back the Perspex panel of the cockpit and raised the thumb of his leather-gloved left hand. Gavin returned the signal.

The rope tautened. Gansenheimer concentrated on the controls. The C-47 was picking up speed. Ahead, another transport plane was airborne, towing slow supply gliders behind it, bobbing and ducking on the thermals. Gavin crossed his fingers for luck.

The Gansenheimer towplane was gathering speed now. The Waco trundled after it clumsily. A sudden growling roar of metal anguish. The C-47 was airborne. Gansenheimer's Waco, jerked from zero to eighty miles an hour in a couple of seconds, rose into the air. Gavin caught his breath. It was bouncing and swaying wildly. Had Gansenheimer lost control? Many glider pilots did at this crucial stage. He had not. The glider continued to rise. Behind it another tow-and-glider took off – and another. Abruptly, as the darkness started to clear and to the east the sun rose, a blood-red ball hanging on the lip of the horizon, as if undecided whether it should continue any further, the dawn sky was full of planes, surging purposefully forward towards the battlefield.

Gavin took one last look, said a quick prayer and hurried back to his jeep, Joe Gansenheimer, the boy pilot, forgotten already. It was the way of war and command. You sent your men to battle – and possible death – and if you were lucky you forgot them. It was the only way.

Now the sirens shattered the morning calm all the fifty miles or so along the river line from Saarburg to Wittlich. Everywhere as the gleaming silver Vs of the Flying Fortresses and Liberators appeared, ready to kill, maim and destroy from two miles up, the flak guns took up the challenge; while the teenage kids, boys and girls, manning the 20mm quadruple anti-aircraft quick firers, swung their light guns back and forth, ready for the back-up that they knew would soon come: the feared *Jabos*, the Ami Lightnings and Mustangs which would support the heavy bomber fleet.

They didn't have to wait long. Even before the 8th Air Force men from England started to drop their loads of sudden death and destruction, the fighter-bombers came sweeping in at tree-top height, jumping over hedges, zipping below bridges and telegraph wires, skidding along the surface of the Sauer, Saar, Moselle like some monstrous silver waterbugs.

Immediately the fifteen- and sixteen-year-olds in their outsize steel helmets took up the challenge. They swung their deadly four 20mm cannons, each of which could fire a thousand shells a minute – no wonder the Americans called them 'the meat choppers' – and faced the intruders. A sheer white wall of flying tracer erupted at once. Still the young pilots braved that tremendous fire. They came in, cannon and machine guns crackling violently, electrically, the length of their wings, sweeping and serving, flying at tree-top height, trying to avoid that terrible killing fire.

A plane was hit. It staggered in mid-air as if it had run into an invisible wall. For an instant it was suspended there, as if nothing had happened. A moment later it erupted in a ball of terrible pink flame. Out of the inferno a single wing fell, turning round and round like a great metal leaf as it floated to the water. Another pressed forward. The pilot, face distorted, grimacing like a man suddenly gone mad, pressed home his attack. A vicious burst of fire raise towards a gunpit. An interested observer would have been able to see the slugs striking up angry spurts of blue sparks as the bullets came ever closer. Next moment they had saturated the pit with their deadly fire. As the plane zoomed overhead at tree-top height, lashing the ground below with its prop wash, the pit exploded in flame, flinging the screaming kids playing soldier to all sides, dead before their bullet-riddled bodies hit the ground.

More planes came zipping out of the sky. They braved that hellish fire, carried away by the crazy bloodlust of war that sees no danger. Gunpits exploded. Young men and women, dying as they did so, crawled from their shattered smoking pits, dragging their cruelly smashed limbs behind them to die alone and forgotten in the snowbound hedges and ditches. Planes went down. One after another. Great smoking plumes, flecked with cherry-red flames, screeching towards the earth in that one last dive of death.

Men went mad. Pilots shrieked at their own reflections in the polished Perspex. Gunners stood on the tops of the devasted gunpits waving their fists at planes, even as the tracer beat a furious path of imminent death in their direction. Horses, which had towed the guns into position, ran frantically back and forth, their manes on fire, bodies lathered in sweat and streaks of crimson where the bullets had struck. Pondorous oxen, used for the same purpose, died slowly and gently in the same manner that they had lived, in unprotesting submission.

Now the *jabos*, their fuel tanks virtually empty, their flying time about used up, started to turn westwards in tight curves, dragging their great evil shadows behind them on the snowfields as they headed for their Belgian bases, their murderous task completed for this day. For by now, most of the light flak was shattered, as the heavy bombers came roaring in in their mighty silver Vs to complete the work of sudden death and destruction. Now it was up to the heavy flak, the great 88mms, manned by trained *Wehrmacht* artillerymen to protect the target cities.

Frau Kreisleiter Schmeer took her left breast out of her blouse and tendered Sergeant Schulze, who was bemused by so much flesh, her offering, simpering in a little girl's voice, "You may suck, dear *Oberscharführer* Schulze, if you so wish." She pointed the great dun-coloured nipple at his face, as if she were pointing an offensive weapon at the SS NCO.

"Holy mackerel," Schulze whispered in sudden awe, "all that meat and no potatoes." He hesitated.

She interpreted his hesitation as shyness and said coyly, moving over closer so the springs of the sofa creaked audibly in protest at the shift in her great weight, "Don't be afraid, my beloved. Mummy will see that everything is all right. You can rely on Mummy to make her little boy happy." She smiled winningly at him.

'Mummy's little boy's frigging well gonna cough up his cookies at any moment now,' the hard little voice at the back of Sergeant Schulze's mind rasped cynically.

"I'm not . . . used to such . . . perversions," Schulze managed to stutter. "I'm a straight meat-an-tatie man." He swallowed hard, twisting fast to avoid that great hanging milky-white dug.

She gripped his crotch through his trousers and was startled at what she found there – or the lack of it. "I can see what you mean," she said, disappointment all too audible in her voice. "But Mummy'll soon take care of it." He could see now that she had a faint trace of a moustache underneath the powder-mask and there were tiny droplets of sweat glistening on the fine hairs. His desire started to ebb ever more quickly. This had been a bad move, a very had one, he told himself. 'Mummy' wasn't going to work out as he had imagined that dawn.

But for once Sergeant Schulze, master of the Hamburg Equaliser, SS farter *par excellence*, was wrong. 'Mummy' still had a few surprises left for him.

With amazing speed and agility for such a gross woman, the *Frau Kreisleiter* wriggled out of her tent-like skirt and tugged hard at her under skirt, which came off immediately, to reveal enormous, fat legs clad in sheer black stockings (the *Kreisleiter* in one of his more amorous moods had brought a dozen pairs of the stockings back with him from an 'inspection trip' during which he caught an unfortunate social disease so the sheer black stockings were never used – at least for his benefit). "Now, my dear darling boy," she cooed, "what do you say to that?"

Aghast, Schulze took in that mountain of naked, white flesh, broken by the black silk, which unfortunately could not hide the fact that the *Frau Kreisleiter* was suffering from a bad case of cellulitis.

"*Himmler fur Führer*!" he uttered the ultimate blasphemy for which he could have been shot without trial anywhere else but the SS. He cowered back on the couch, hands in front of his shocked, ashen face like small children do when they want to blot out some horror almost beyond bearing.

The *Frau Kreisleiter* did not seem to notice. Perhaps she was carried away by her own burning passion. "Now," she said, like a patient mother with an awkward child, "I shall see that you are made happy."

Schulze remembered how he had once burned for her body in what now seemed another age (in fact it had been the night before) and told himself he had been crazy: I mustn't have had all my cups in the cupboard. How could he have thought he would sacrifice his body and that precious length of flesh dangling between his legs – that thought stopped him short. What if this was the beginning of the end? *What if he were never able to get it up ever again*? He'd have to kill himself. And it seemed, as that half-naked monster pumped away at his flaccid organ without any effect, that he would have to face up to that eventuality. Nothing was working!

"Never mind," she cried as the drone of the approaching bombers grew ever louder. "Love will conquer all."

"What in three devils' name are you going to do?" Schulze cried in alarm, as she raised her massive haunch with a grunt and a squeak of a rusty garter strap. "You can't . . ." He cowered with sudden alarm, as she raised herself and moved in on his loins. "You'll crush me. Take care, woman—"

The rest of his words were drowned by a great groan, as she descended upon his stomach with her full weight, an unholy look, almost one of dementia, in her bloodshot eyes.

It was then, as *Frau Kreisleiter* Schmeer started to pump her black-clad lower body up and down on Schulze's crushed form that the first bomb struck home some fifty metres away. The house hit came tumbling and rumbling down in a great spurt of dust and shattered masonry, as *Frau* Schmeer cried with delight, "It's working, my beloved . . . It's working . . . Mummy's doing it for you . . . I swear I just felt the earth move . . ."

A moment or two later the 'earth moved again', as the second bomb struck home with a thunderous roar. This time the earth moved all too drastically. The wall opposite the couch flew apart, taking with it the Führer's picture and that of *Kreisleiter* Schmeer, hand clutching his ceremonial Storm Troopers' dagger, to reveal to the outside world running for shelter from the raid the amazing twosome engaged in that monstrous coupling of theirs, which would undoubtedly have shocked even that arch-lecher, Minister of Propaganda and Public Enlightenment Dr Josef Goebbels.

It certainly shocked *Kreisleiter* Schmeer, who once in his best years had struck that heroic pose in his SA uniform, complete with dagger. He paused in mid-stride, the danger momentarily forgotten, the vinegar-soaked bandanna slipping down the side of his fat face, and stared at the sight with unblinking amazement.

And there was certainly something to stare at. Appearing like a vision painted by Rubens, through the smoke of war, two huge people lay, mouths gaping open stupidly with shock, bodies nearly naked, with the woman, who was his very own wife, bulging naked flesh everywhere above the sheer silk black stockings, astride the male, jerking herself back and forth as if she were riding a very frisky stallion, her hand raised to strike its flank and urge it to go ever faster.

"Christ on a frigging crutch," Corporal Matz, standing stupefied behind the flabbergasted Party official, whispered in awe, "like a frigging fiddler's elbow."

That phrase broke the spell. "I'll give him frigging fiddler's elbow!" Schmeer cried, face brick-red with sudden rage. "Doesn't he knew that he's slipping a link to a friend of the Führer, proud possessor of the War Service Cross First Class – I'll have the balls off'n him with a blunt razor-blade, I swear I will."

It was at that precise moment that Sergeant Schulze felt that delightful old urge pulsating in his hitherto useless loins. Perhaps it was the sudden shock that had done it. He raised himself. Impaled as she was, *Frau Kreisleiter* Schmeer was forced to rise with him. Schulze, still blinded by dust and not recognising the *Kreisleiter*, clenched a fist like a small steam shovel and bellowed, "Let no one speak thus of my fiancée. Or by the Great Whore of Buxtehude where the dogs piss through their ribs, I'll polish his visage for him so hard that he'll be looking out at the world from his asshole."

That terrible curse and threat did it. As outraged as he was, *Kreisleiter* Schmeer knew when he was beaten. "That's done it," he snapped at the grinning soldiers, as Corporal Matz started to laugh, a laugh that would be soon taken up by half a hundred young soldiers. "I'm slinging me hook. She's not the only bit o' gash in the knocking shop." Red with fury, he pushed his way through the grinning, laughing throng of SS troopers, who still stared pop-eyed at the amazing scene before them, as Sergeant Schulze attempted to untangle his pubic hair from *Frau Kreisleiter* Schmeer's metal garter clips. He flung open the door of his Opel Blitz, pausing only on the running board to cry like some heroic tenor at the end of a moving, emotional scene, "I am going to another place. I shall never return, woman, after this treachery." And with that he departed for the comforts of the hill and the Camp Commandant's intimate little Christmas Eve party, leaving the laughing throng and a still surprised Schulze behind. Schulze and his dedicated search for the 'eternal womanhood' (though the big NCO didn't put it exactly like that)* had set the ball rolling. What had started in knock-about farce would end in deepest tragedy . . .

"Phew," Spiv breathed out hard, face greased with sweat although he was still freezing cold, "cor ferk a duck! That was ruddy close." He pushed aside the wrecked door of the little bunker on the hill and nearly stumbled over the corpse of a dead elderly German soldier, his dental plate bulging out of his gaping mouth like a set of horse teeth.

Behind him the rest of Mallory's Marauders skidded to a halt, as to the West the last of the Flying Fortresses droned away, their task completed for this day. Later, their pilots would distribute presents for English kids, along with the squadron leader, padded with cushions and dressed as a benign Father Christmas and plenty of hearty 'ho-ho-ho's' for the press photographer of the *Stars & Stripes*, the US Army newspaper. It was that kind of war.

Mallory nodded to Peters and Kitchener. "Get rid of him," he snapped, catching his breath, his gaze already fixed on the POW camp next to the burning barracks below.

* *das ewige Weib* in German.

Sprawled next to Mallory, who was now surveying the camp through an adapted pair of binoculars prepared specially for his one good eye, Spiv asked, "How we gonna spot this brasshat of yours, sir? There must be hundreds of Yank POWs down there. The place is swarming with them." He indicated the groups of Kriegies emerging from the camp's shelters under the watchful eyes of the handful of middle-aged guards.

"I have a photo of the General, of course, Spiv," Mallory agreed. "But I don't think the Huns would like us to go noseying around, asking after Brigadier Horowitz. Once the balloon goes up—"

"Balloon goes up?"

"Yes, it's obvious. We've got to start trouble, let the Yanks break out – they vastly outnumber the guards as you can definitely see – and then we'll ask our questions. Time will be of the essence. We'll have to make the DZ rendezvous before dark. If we don't . . ." He left the rest of his sentence unfinished.

"Then we'll be up to our hooters in shit – up the frigging creek without a paddle, sir."

"You may phrase it like that, Spiv," Mallory said mildly as he continued his surveillance of the camp, which had been saved from the bombing probably due to the large announcement painted on the roof of the camp commandant's office, announcing, 'ALLIED POW CAMP. ATTENTION!'

He told himself the wire next to the watchtower at the furthest end of hexagon from the commandant's office would be the best place to begin the break-in. There was only a single machine gunner in the tower and his view to the outside was obstructed by a snow-heavy tree which blocked his field of fire. Next to the base of the tower were the electric generator boxes. They probably controlled the camp's lights and possibly, if the wire *were* electrified, the electrification of the triple-wire perimeter fence. Knock that out and there would be little to stop a mass exodus of the POWs.

Spiv, embued with that native cockney East End cunning of his, seemed to read Mallory's mind, for he queried, "Sir, if we can get the poor Yankee sods out, which I suppose we can, what we gonna do with them afterwards? You know yersen, what dipsticks the Yanks are when they ain't got nobody to lead 'em. Most of 'em couldn't find their way into a knocking shop with a big white fiver in their hand."

Mallory grinned, though at that particular moment he had never felt less like grinning; the situation was much too serious. After all, Horowitz knew a secret that might well prolong the duration of the bloody war right into 1947 – and he knew in his bones the British Empire wouldn't survive that long if it had to continue fighting a major war with the ever-declining resources at the great Empire's disposal. "Good question," he answered after a moment's thought. He sighed. "I'm afraid the great majority of the Yanks'll just have to look after themselves. We can't take all of them with us, I fear."

"Me heart bleeds for 'em," Spiv said with a crooked grin.

"Cynic," Mallory countered, and then he forgot the mass of the Yank POWs for Peters suddenly hissed, "There's a car coming up the road hell-for-leather, sir. Hope it don't mean trouble for us?"

"Don't blow a gasket," Spiv mocked. "How the hellus would they knew we're here, you great soft pudden?"

"Shut up. I can't hear myself think," Mallory ordered, switching his glass to the civilian car speeding up the hill towards the POW camp, the rubber gas bag on its roof which supplied the Opel's engine with fuel wobbling back and forth like some great blackcurrant jelly.

At the gate, the guard commander lined up his middle-aged soldiers. They snapped to attention, their rifles at the ready. "Someone important," Mallory told himself, wondering idly if Spiv was right after all. He followed the car's slow progress inside the compound, the driver honking his horn at the POWs to get out of his way until finally the Opel came to a halt in front of the main building and a fat man in uniform emerged and waddled self-importantly inside. "A Party official," Mallory announced to nobody in particular. "Wonder what he's here for on Christmas Eve?"

"Do you think, sir, his nibs is—" Spiv commenced once more, but Mallory shut him up almost immediately with a terse, "All right, we've got our wind back. I think we ought to get closer to that watchtower and see what we can do."

Behind him Thaelmann, the veteran of such camps himself, snapped in his heavy accent, "Sir, the guards will be facing inward. It is normal. They expect no trouble from the outside. But there can be other things of danger on the outside to make up for their failings."

"Oh, piss or get off the pot," Spiv snarled. "What d'yer frigging mean, mate, other things of danger?"

But Thaelmann was not to be drawn. His hard, heavy, sombre face revealed nothing. All he would say was: "Care must be taken . . . you never know with the damned fascists."

And Thaelmann proved to be right. Ten minutes later they were in position, crouched in the snow-heavy firs some fifty yards away from the stork-legged tower, with above them, glimpsed through the fringes of dark green, the sky turning from hard blue to an ugly menacing green, indicating that fresh snowfall was soon on its way. Hardly daring to breathe, glad when any noise from the camp covered the sounds they made as they lay full length in the frozen snow surveying the the tower, they took stock of the place. They were all professionals in this business. Without any unnecessary discussion they worked out the angle of approach; how they should conceal themselves if the guard on the tower (who was currently smoking secretly, hand cupped around the glowing end of his cigarette in the fashion of sentries all over the world) should turn in their direction; how they should deal with the unsuspecting guard when they nobbled him, and so on. For all of them knew that if the guard above them could sound the alarm in time they didn't stand a chance in hell of getting away safely. And what would come thereafter, if they were all captured, was all too obvious.

As Spiv snorted when the subject was raised, "Yer don't have to draw me a frigging picture in oil, Peters. They'll put us against the nearest wall and – *bang* – there goes yer frigging head! . . . Bob's yer frigging uncle."

"But we're in uniform," Kitchener objected.

Mildly, Mallory shook his head. "That won't matter at this stage of the war. Because we're behind their lines that'll be enough for the Huns. As Spiv here has just said in his normal silver-tongued manner it'll be bang and Bob's yer uncle—"

The words froze on his lips. Behind them there was a soft footfall on the frozen crust of the snow. Abruptly his nostrils were assailed by an unpleasant, raunchy animal smell.

"What is it?" Thaelmann spotted the sudden look of alarm on Mallory's battered face.

Mallory didn't answer. He held his finger to his lips in warning and cocking his head to one side, listened intently.

The others did the same, hearts abruptly beating furiously like trip-hammers, hands clenched into sweaty, damp fists.

For a moment or two, Mallory thought he had imagined the soft footfall in the trees behind them. But no. There it was again; and this time it was clear and definite. He opened his mouth and mouthed the urgent warning: 'D . . . o . . . n . . . t . . . s . . . h . . . o . . . o . . . t.' His hand slipped down to the commando knife at his side. Automatically the others did the same. The footfall came closer. Mallory started to sweat hard. *What the hell was out there?*

Next moment he knew.

A huge furry cross between a Doberman and an Alsatian poked its ugly snout out from the trees and stared hard at the little group of men crouched petrified in front of him. It did not seem to comprehend why they were there; it was as if it could not believe the evidence of its own sick-yellow eyes.

Carefully, very carefully, keeping his face expressionless for some reason he could not quite understand, Commander Mallory slipped his fingers into the brass knuckles of the commando fight knife and prepared for what *had* to come. Even that slight noise caught the brute's attention. Its ears jerked up instantly, as it swivelled its long snout to see what Mallory was up to.

"Watch it, sir," Spiv muttered *sotto voce*; there was no mistaking the fear in his tone now.

Mallory didn't respond. He daren't. Now he concentrated his whole body, his every sense on the half-wild guard dog. The animal seemed to be doing the same. It crouched slowly – very slowly – on to its powerful hindlegs, baring its fetid, yellow fangs.

A fearful Kitchener gasped something in Arabic. Thaelmann cursed in a choked voice. Peters whispered, "Let him jump, sir, if it wants to. I'll handle him. I was brought up with dogs."

The animal didn't like that talk. A growl started deep down inside its throat. It grew louder and ever more menacing. Mallory felt the small hairs at the back of his head grow erect. The beast was about to spring. He realised that with the sudden one hundred per cent certainty of a vision. His hand gripping the commando knife was abruptly wet with sweat. Suddenly he felt helpless. He'd drop the knife; he knew he would.

Now the guard dog was crouched on its haunches. Its ears were tucked neatly along the length of its skull. Foam dripped from the sides of its powerful, frightening jaws. It was now . . .

"*Get him, sir!*" Peters yelled in alarm as the dog launched itself forward from the crouched position. Desperately Mallory lashed out with his sharp blade. He missed. Next instant he tumbled down, the dog on top of him, his nostrils full of the dog's animal stench, foam splattering his face.

He stabbed forward again. He felt his blade sink into the

animal's hide. It yelped with pain and ripped the length of Mallory's face with its razor-sharp claws. Instinctively he reached out his free hand and clamped it around the dog's muzzle.

It writhed and wriggled frantically to break the hold. Just as frantically, Mallory, being tossed thither and hither by the immensely powerful beast, hung on. He must prevent it barking and alarming the guard just above them.

"Let me, sir," Peters hissed.

Mallory felt Peters scramble across his inert body.

Peters didn't hesitate. His big right hand shot out. It found the dog's testicles. His fingers gripped them and pressed hard. The beast whined. Desperately it twisted and turned in an attempt to break that crushing grip. With all his strength Peters hung on, beads of sweat streaming down his brick-red face like opaque pearls. Through gritted teeth, he ordered, "Get his muzzle, sir. NOW!"

Mallory hesitated an instant. Then he broke his hold and grabbed the dog's jaws and hung on. Frantic now with the pain in its testicles and its breathing being cut off, the hound whirled and twisted, taking the two burly Englishmen with it as it did so. Time and time again it lashed out with its claws.

By now Mallory and Peters were lathered in sweat, their faces bleeding where the half-crazed hound had slashed their cheeks with its wildly flailing claws. All the same they knew they had to deal with it soon. Any minute now the guard on the top of the tower would spot the crazy fight in the firs and then the shooting would commence.

Mallory attempted to gasp out an order, but Peters beat him to it. He choked for breath and gasped, "It's bloody . . . jaw . . . Break its jaw . . ."

Mallory acted. He had never done anything like it before. But he knew the way he had to do it. It was going to be a mixture of split-second timing and sheer brute strength. He forced himself to control his breathing, counted three under his breath and then let go. The dog gasped for air and opened its snout, yellow fangs dripping saliva, to bark. It was then that Mallory, with the last of his strength, grasped both the animal's upper and lower jaw and pulled apart with every last ounce of energy he could summon.

The beast's spine arched like a taut bow. Peters hung on to its genitals as they seemed about to slip from his grasp, his eyes bulging out of their sockets like those of a madman. Mallory exerted more pressure. A low keening started within the dying beast which grew louder. Mallory, frantic that they would be discovered by the noise, forced himself to tug harder. His arms were on fire with the effort. His breath was coming in sharp, hectic gasps. It was as if he were running a great race.

The hound gave one last electric twitch. It ran through the length of its tortured, pain-racked body. "Hang on, sir," Peters urged frantically. "Hang on—" The plea died on his lips. The hound lay suddenly still. For what seemed an age the little group of desperate men stared at the furry shape stretched out in the scuffed snow, blood curling in a black trickle from the side of its snout. The fearsome beast had suddenly been transformed into what looked like a bundle of abandoned furry rags.

Slowly, infinitely slowly, as if they were still not certain the hound was dead, Mallory and Peters relinquished their grasp, their hands now stiff and unfeeling. They stared down at the furry shape. Was it really dead? Spiv did the honours for them. With the tip of his heavy boot, he aimed a hefty kick at the animal's ribs. A solid thud. Nothing. The dog didn't move. It really was dead.

Dizzy and numb, Mallory clambered to his feet like an old man suffering from rheumatics. He stared down at the dog. They all did. There was a heavy silence over the group that seemed to reign for ever. In the end, Mallory said in a voice that he hardly recognised as his own, "Bury the dog . . . We'd better see about the guard in the tower." Without another word, he turned and trudged forward towards the camp.

*   *   *

It was like all the wartime stations that von Dodenburg ever remembered seeing over the last five years: couples clinging to each other like shipwrecked victims fearing to be drowned; hard-eyed chaindogs* watching the soldiers, carbines slung over their heavy shoulders, as if they suspected each and every one of the 'stubble hoppers' of being a deserter; important officials and officers striding back and forth with their clipboards and indelible pencils, doing what such people did; engines letting off great clouds of steam and chattering noisily as if impatient to be off to the great adventure of war; whores in the shadows, giving excited, urgent soldiers hand-jobs or (for an extra price) allowing them the strenuous sexual pleasure of the 'butterfly'. All was as von Dodenburg remembered a score of such leave-takings, save that now, in Trier's grossly damaged *Hauptbahnhof*, the bombastic military music of the good years no longer played over the loudspeakers and those harsh, distorted, metallic announcements, which revealed the extent of Germany's New Empire, no longer gave the arrival and departure of troop trains to Smolensk, Kiev, Warsaw, Paris, Brussels and the like. The wheels that had once 'rolled for victory', as the slogans of the good years had proclaimed, now rolled for defeat.

Not that such matters concerned the girl. She was totally concerned with him – and naturally herself, as the star-crossed lover. Cynical beyond her years, he told himself, she was still a nice, if silly and self-centred, girl, who believed at this moment that her world was falling apart.

Carrying her rucksack, though it was forbidden for officers to carry things in their hands in public, he led her across the floor littered with shattered glass to where the trains awaited. The Christmas tree which had adorned the entrance had been blown down by the early raid, its few

* German military policemen, so called because of the metal plates of their office they wore round their necks.

empty, gaily coloured parcels scattered everywhere. Even the papier-mâché angel which had been placed on the tip of the tree had been squashed underfoot in the dawn panic, unnoticed.

They approached the barrier. As usual there were the two chaindogs and a middle-aged civilian in ankle-length leather coat, cigar clamped between his gold teeth, who had Gestapo written all over him, waiting there to check ID cards and travel documents. Von Dodenburg joined the queue of soldiers, burdened with rifles and equipment, silent, sad losers the lot of them – cannon-fodder, von Dodenburg noted automatically – and shabby, smelly civilians, frightened out of their lives, fleeing Trier while they still had a chance to do so.

Von Dodenburg held out his pass and the ticket to Koblenz which he had obtained for the girl at a substantial bribe. The Gestapo man nodded and the two chaindogs clicked to attention. They knew the notoriously short fuse of arrogant young officers of the SS, especially the likes of this one, a colonel already and his skinny chest covered with tin of every variety.

The Gestapo man wasn't impressed, though. After all he was Gestapo. He had served the Kaiser, the Republic, the Führer and he would probably survive Josef Stalin when the Soviet dictator took over Germany soon. The main thing was he survived to receive his pension. He looked at the girl. "*Fraulein* . . . er . . . Schmeer," he said, rolling his stump of cheap cigars from one side of his slack mouth to the other, "you haven't got special permission to travel on this train, you know. What d'yer say to that?" He looked hard at her.

Von Dodenburg waited, avoiding eye contact with the officious cop, though he could feel the chaindogs watching him beneath the brims of their steel helmets wondering when he would explode. He promised the fat cop silently that that wouldn't take long.

"*Fraulein*, this train is reserved for the troops and genuine refugees from the bombing who possess a certificate from the Burgomaster's office." The Gestapo looked severely at the pale-faced girl, who was sobbing again.

Voice thick with tears, she quavered, "I don't want to go . . . he's making me go." She tugged von Dodenburg's sleeve and looked up at him, damp eyes full of everlasting love.

The cop looked from one to the other and seemingly took in the situation in a flash; after all he had been born to expect the worst from his fellow human beings. That's why he had survived. "Are you friends, *Obersturmbannführer*?" he asked. The way that he emphasised the word 'friends' revealed the way he was thinking.

Von Dodenburg felt his temper rising. He dropped his hand to his pistol holster significantly. It didn't seem to worry the Gestapo man. He said, "There seems to be a – er – rather large age difference, if I may say so."

Haughtily, coldly, dangerously, he looked the Gestapo man up and down as if he were something exceedingly unpleasant that had just crawled out from the sewers and said icily, "You're risking a fat lip, aren't you?"

The Gestapo's pudgy pale face flushed red. "I say—"

He didn't get the chance to finish. For von Dodenburg grabbed him by the lapels so that the green leather coat squeaked audibly and hissed, "Get out of my way, you fat shit, if you value your life. I've shot rear-echelon stallions like you before breakfast many a time. Now – *move*!"

The Gestapo man moved and shouldering her pack once more, von Dodenburg passed the barrier, holding her tightly to his side. Someone at the back of the crowd of hushed, timid civilians clapped.

Now they stood on the damp platform, both shivering a little, not with emotion but with the icy wind that blew in straight from Siberia. She was still crying, muttering in between sobs, "Oh, don't make me go, Kuno . . . I'll never see you again . . . I can't bear it . . ." She looked up at him desperately. "I'll die, I swear I will . . . Oh, don't leave me."

He looked down at her calmly. She was going to her aunt at Guls on the other side of the Moselle from Koblenz. She would be safe there from the bombs and probably from the Ami guns when they attacked across the Rhine soon. He had forced her to give him the address. "Of course, you'll live," he said. "You'll be alive long after I've gone."

"Don't say that, Kuno," she hushed fearfully.

He laughed. "It's a fact of life. In fifty years' time when you're old and a granny, you might recall me – *very vaguely* – and wonder what all the fuss was about. You'll probably laugh and tell yourself what a silly girl you were when you were young—"

"But I love you *now*," she interrupted fervently, pressing his arm so hard that it actually hurt.

"Love," he mocked. "Oh, love!"

Up ahead, the locomotive started to clatter in, its cylinder covered with branches as camouflage, its tender riddled with bright silver spots where the metal had been machine-gunned by enemy *jabos*. A cry rose from the waiting mob, almost animal with desire and relief. "The train," von Dodenburg said. He pushed her forward and the crowd parted obediently before the high-ranking SS officer.

"Kuno—"

"Get in." He pushed that delightful little rump up the steel steps, feeling the hot flesh beneath the thin cheap material of her Hitler Maiden skirt. As he did so, he wondered what she would be like when he was dead. Would all that drive, that fervour, that passion have vanished by then, when she was an ordinary housewife with kids, worrying about how to stretch the weekly budget in a world at peace – a normal world?

He grinned. It was a world he couldn't conceive of with the best of wills. He had never known such an existence and he never would; he had been doomed to war and battle. When that was over, he'd be finished too.

She looked down at him from the open window, as more and more civilians pushed on to the train, clambering up on the roof, fighting for whatever small space they could call their own, while fat perspiring officials cursed and yelled, trying to retain some order in the growing chaos. Up front, the locomotive steamed and puffed. Impatiently the station master with his peaked red cap and leather crossband, which made him look like a nineteenth-century cavalryman, waited for his staff to get the doors of the long, packed train closed.

"Will you remember, at least, Kuno?" she asked gently.

It was that fatal typical German sentimentality, he told himself. All the same it was a little touching, even sad. "Of course," he answered resolutely.

"For ever?"

"For ever," he lied.

"*Turen schliessen*," the station master bellowed above the racket, raising his signal disc, "*der D-Zug nach Koblenz hat bald Abfahrt!*"

Von Dodenburg stepped back. Up front, the locomotive's steel wheels chattered as they attempted to find purchase on the slick tracks. Steam rose, enveloping the figure of the station master, with his whistle in his mouth, so that he looked like some Wagnerian heroic figure, glimpsed through a stage mist.

"Kuno!" she cried desperately, the tears streaming down her young face.

"Look after yourself," he cried back, mind already full of what was to come once this Christmas Eve was over.

A whistle shrilled. Voices rose in parting. Shuddering, slipping, the long train started to move. Someone fainted unnoticed. The station master sighed. He tucked his disc under his right arm, as *Reichsbahn* regulations prescribed. Kuno von Dodenburg caught one last glimpse of her face at the window. Then an unshaven soldier pushed her out of the way and began waving furiously at someone on the platform.

The train started to gather speed. A whistle shrilled. It echoed back and forth in the barren cavern of the station. The train began to curve out of the station. Two tail lights glowed red. A final whistle and it was gone.

The Gestapo man glowered at von Dodenburg as he passed through the barrier once more, but Von Dodenburg ignored him. Indeed he had already forgotten that fat cop, as he was beginning to forget the events of the last hour. It had to be that way with front swine, as he was. Nothing was permanent. As Corporal Matz would have put it regarding 'love': "It's all four Fs, sir . . ." Here he would chirp, "Find 'em, feel 'em, fuck 'em and forget 'em." Crude indeed, but what did front swine expect from their short, violent, brutal lives?

He passed into the open where the captured jeep was waiting for him. The young driver took his eyes off the shapely, frozen legs of the pavement pounder smoking in the shadows, waiting for another customer, and started up. "Won't be long now, sir," he said cheerfully.

"What won't be long?"

The driver looked at him out of the corner of his eyes. "Why, sir, the Wotan piss-up, sir. After all it *is* Christmas Eve."

"Of course, of course," von Dodenburg agreed hastily. He didn't want to spoil the boy's sense of anticipation.

They started to move away, heading for the Porta Nigra and then down to the river. At the *Romerbrucke*, the weary, red-eyed lieutenant in charge of the flak cannon rose hastily to his feet, called his teenage gunners to attention and saluted.

Von Dodenburg touched the peak of his battered cap carelessly and said, "Stand at ease, Lieutenant. Rest the weary bones."

"Thank you, sir."

Von Dodenburg smiled. "Happy Christmas to you and your brave fellows."

"Again thank you, sir." The Lieutenant beamed. "It wasn't every day that a *Wehrmacht* gunner was called 'brave fellow' by an SS officer. "And Happy Christmas to you, sir."

Von Dodenburg nodded. Above him the lone enemy plane glided silently to its landing place totally unnoticed . . .

*   *   *

"*Quiet in the knocking shop!*" Sergeant Schulze bellowed in high good humour, recovered now from the unhappy episode of the morning, though unfortunately *Frau Kreisleiter* Schmeer was not. It was said that the nuns had her strapped to a bed upstairs, and after giving her extreme unction were spraying her with Holy Water, blessed by the Archbishop of Trier personally, every two hours.

Matz, who was in on the little plot, winked. Schulze winked back, red-faced and full of good humour and plentiful additions of suds and firewater. "Comrades," he said, appealing for silence with both paws raised, "let's have a bit o' decorum. If you don't know what that means, I'll tell yer. Hold yer water or I'll twist yer piss-cannon till yer glassy orbits pop outa their sockets!"

That terrible oath did it. The happy, already slight drunk young troopers fell silent and stared up to the head of the festivally decorated table, complete with Christmas tree and contraceptives hanging from it, colourfully and tastefully filled with sundry liqueurs.

"Now, let's remember we're in Catholic Trier, where the Pope in Rome comes to buy his yearly ration of wine from the nuns – and other things." He gave them the benefit of a huge, knowing wink and they laughed dutifully. They always laughed at Senior Sergeant Schulze's pathetic attempts at humour. It would have been very unwise, possibly even dangerous, not to have done so. "So we've got to have a bit of hush and not too much firewater till the Archbishop and his nuns have been to bless us." He lowered his head reverently and folded his hands in front in front of his bulging crotch, as if at a moment of silent prayer.

Matz looked suitably pious until he was caught short by the litre of green pea soup that he had eaten earlier on to 'fortify' himself and had to rip off a tremendous fart, which had the troopers all around grabbing at their throats as if they were choking, and crying in stifled voices, "Gas attack . . . on with yer masks."

"All right, all right, you bunch o' fart-cannons, enough of that. I think there's just time for a little drink before the Bishop arrives. I won't bother to say grace, if you don't mind." He raised the ornate chamber pot in front of him, filled with good Munich beer that somewhat obscured the portrait of Winston Churchill which adorned its inner bottom, and toasted, "Up the cups, comrades. The night's gonna be cool."

"Up the cups. The night's gonna be cool," a couple of hundred happy voices echoed his words eagerly, minds full of the great piss-up to come, though their young minds didn't know at that moment that it was going to be, on the contrary, a very hot night indeed.

Mallory stepped over the dead guard, Kitchener's knife still quivering in his back, and flashed a quick look at the camp. It was unusually noisy for some reason, he told himself, but otherwise everything seemed to be normal. Perhaps the Kriegies were getting an extra ration of food and alcohol this Christmas Eve day? He dismissed the matter and got down to business. Time was running out fast. By now the glider would have landed. They had perhaps another three hours left to reach it with the General before night fell.

"Gun, Spiv," he commanded.

"Stevens, Thaelmann – the generators."

"You, Kitchener, start clipping the wire."

Like the well-trained soldiers they were, they needed no further instructions. In addition, all of them knew as well that time was of the essence. They couldn't waste a minute. Rapidly they set about their task, the icy December air suddenly full of the almond-stink of the plastic explosive they were using to mine the wire, generators and the like.

Mallory, moving back and forth across the deck of the guard tower, trying to penetrate the wooden walls of the Kriegies' huts nodded his approval. There might only be a handful of his Marauders, but they were worth a hundred conventional soldiers. Besides, soon they'd have the overwhelming numbers of the freed POWs on their side. Slowly he started to feel they'd pull off the op, after all. They'd better . . .

The Kriegies were drunk. But not in that happy manner one would have expected this festive day with the prospect of a better new year and freedom just around the corner. No, they were mean drunk, resentful at being behind barbed wire this Christmas Eve, prepared to make anyone – and everyone – pay for the wrongs they believed had been done to them. In short, they were out for blood.

Now the huts shook with drunken singing – they had stolen sugar and raisins from the camp's store, made a potent brew out of the two ingredients, and added the mix to the barrel of cheap Moselle wine the Camp Commandant had given them. But in the case of the six or seven Kriegies hiding this dark afternoon in the stinking crapper, it had not improved their mood. Indeed it had worsened it if anything. Their red-rimmed eyes were full of mayhem and murder and when they whispered to one another in their hiding place behind the '28-seater', their conversation was replete with cusswords and dire threats.

Earlier on they had already torn up the unwashed, stained boards of the rearmost crappers, a couple of them nearly falling drunkenly into the seething, stinking mess below, alive with crawling, wriggling fat white maggots. They had replaced the boards and strewn the bits of packing paper they used as loo paper over the cracks so that they wouldn't be spotted at first sight. After all, what they intended had to be done by *all* of them together – and quickly at that. They wanted no delay for sudden fits of nerves. As 'Green Smoke', the big Texan, had drawled when they had planned it in their huts, "We give him five minutes, guys, at the most. Then we beat it. 'Kay?"

Then they had been sober. Still they had agreed to his murderous plan without hesitation or discussion, for they knew, as the Texan had said earlier, 'We've gotta show the Krauts what we're made of. We're goddam red-blooded Americans – them German bastards aren't gonna push us around much longer, *no siree*!'

Now they waited in tense angry expectation, trying not to notice the stench or the scrabble of the rats' clawed feet on the tin roof of the latrine, with Green Smoke, the only one who still possessed a watch, flashing glances at its green-glowing luminous dial every few minutes. For they knew his schedule well enough; they had had all the time in the world to study it over the last weeks.

'The creep takes tea with the frigging Commandant and that four-eyed peeper of his at three. He passes on the camp scuttlebutt and betrays a few of our guys, the Moxie traitor-bastard. Then they all kiss,' – here Green Smoke had affected a fake falsetto – ''cos they're all faggots, fruitcake to the man.' He had spat contemptuously in the way that only a Texan can spit. 'After, the Moxie gets his orders for the night, takes his goddam bribe and the two Krauts go off duty, probably to play with each others' peckers.' He had spat again. 'By fifteen thirty hours, the Moxie's through. He comes over here to take his usual piss and then . . .' he had left the rest of the sentence unspoken, but they had needed no further explanation. Each one of them had the details of what would happen then engraved on their angry hearts.

"*The Moxie!*" The lookout's urgent whisper from outside cut into their thoughts with electric suddenness.

"Get ready, guys," Green Smoke whispered from his hiding place. He gripped the wire-bound club more firmly in a hand that already was beginning to sweat with tension.

Rosenstein fumbled with his flies in a preoccupied fashion as he entered the gloom of the latrine, his mind full of his plans for this evening. It was virtually all arranged. He'd take Horowitz out, as he had already discussed with the paratroop General. Naturally, Horowitz wouldn't be going back to his own people as he anticipated. The man, typically American with that old Zionist attitude – 'a Zionist is a Jew who pays another Jew to go to Palestine' – wouldn't lift a finger to help the new state that he and his fellows were desperate to create. Horowitz and his ilk (and he'd met a lot of them during his brief stay in the USA as an unwanted refugee from Germany) paid lip service to the future Israel, but that was all. They wanted to live their comfortable bourgeois lives in New York and let other Jews do the hard and dangerous work for them. But Horowitz and the rest would have to learn differently. He finished undoing his flies, wrinkling his nose at the terrible stench coming from the latrines that all the lime and creosote in this world couldn't hide. He stopped short abruptly. There had been a sudden noise, a kind of shuffling, too loud to have been the noise of the rats which were everywhere. He frowned and then one of the hut doors opened and there was a burst of raucous laughter coming from the drunks inside.

"Slobs," he said to himself, "just drunken slobs." He hurried forward, eager to evacuate his bladder and be gone to meet Horowitz; he couldn't stand the stench of the crapper for more than a minute at the most.

A second later, a big smelly hand clapped itself around his mouth and stifled his surprise cry of alarm. "All right, Jewboy," a voice warned, "hold it just there. This is where you get yours, kike . . ."

Horowitz stopped. It was growing increasingly dark now. There was snow in the air. It wouldn't be long now before it started to come down again. He told himself these were ideal conditions for escaping. The men were drunk and he suspected that the guards too were drinking secretly every time they went into the guardroom and the guard commander wasn't looking. He was certain that the CO and that creep of a security officer were celebrating. He could hear a scratchy gramophone playing a tango from the officers' quarters and the occasional clink of glasses. A chink of red light slipped from the nearest blacked-out window. Once he had seen a gross, old Party functionary come staggering through the door to urinate a great yellow steaming stream into the frozen snow. Yes, the brass were having a Christmas Eve party, too; there was now no doubt about that.

He frowned. Suddenly he felt very much alone here in the deserted barracks square with the icy wind blowing across from the east. But where was Sergeant Rosenstein? He was a funny guy in a Central European kind of way and, although he was a fellow Jew, Horowitz didn't altogether trust him. He didn't know why. He shook himself and it wasn't with the cold. Soon the truck would be coming up the hill to the camp to deliver the 'whores', as Rosenstein called them. By then the two of them should be ready to take it. They'd dodge out from beside the latrine as soon as it slowed down to take the final bend. They'd take it there and then before the driver would have time to react. With the stolen pass that Rosenstein said he'd provide, they'd be on their way again back down to the ruined Trier below within half an hour. They'd cross the Moselle and head for France in the little boat Rosenstein said he had stashed away on the eastern bank 'before the Krauts know what's hit 'em' as a very confident Rosenstein had stated. But where was the damned noncom? Angrily, Horowitz gripped the sock, filled with sand to make a primitive blackjack, which was going to be his only weapon.

Where the Sam Hill was Rosenstein? . . . And what was that noise? . . .

Spiv reported back first. His skinny little chest was heaving hectically, but his sharp little cockney eyes were gleaming with excitement. "Done, sir," he gasped and slid down to the floor of the guard room where Mallory squatted next to the MG 42 machine gun. "Wired up the HQ and the fence to the far side . . . Gate no deal. Too risky." The words came out in short-winded, staccato bursts.

"Good show, Spiv," Mallory said. "That's done it as far as you're—"

He didn't finish. Thaelmann had just loomed up out of the growing darkness.

"Sentry far end – nobbled." When he was excited, which wasn't often in such a gloomy, self-disciplined man, he fractured his English a little. "No problem there. Plastic laid . . . It'll wreck ten-twenty metres of wire."

Again Mallory thanked him. Everything was going according to plan. Once the explosions started, the POWs would come streaming out of their huts. Perhaps they might think their compatriots had arrived to free them. At all events, with their lives so boring at the moment, they'd want to see the fun and games, even if there was danger involved. But for him and his Marauders, just a handful of men against the whole Trier garrison, the major problem was picking out General Horowitz from the great mass of prisoners and spiriting him away to the glider before the German reinforcements arrived. It was then Mallory had his brainwave. The solution had been right under his nose all along. He stared past the dead German, already beginning to stiffen in the icy wind, into his cabin. Yes, the apparatus was there and could be used until they cut off the power at the generators. The only problem was whether the General would react to their appeal. After all he was a smart operator. Mallory grinned cynically. "Well, generals were *supposed* to be smart operators. What if Horowitz thought it was some kind of a trick?

But before he could pursue the thought, Peters from below hissed, "Truck coming up sir . . . army."

Mallory started. *Trouble* – the alarming thought shot through his mind. Did the truck signify some new danger?

In the latrines, the desperate Kriegies thought it did. They knew what the slowly approaching truck contained – the whores that their pimp of a prisoner procured for the Kraut brass. Would the latter now need him to help get the panties off the whores? If they did, they'd come looking for him and, as Green Smoke now explained, putting their dread thoughts into words, "*The shit'll hit the fan!*"

He made his decision. Gripping the stake, his only

weapon, more tightly in his horny rancher's hand, he snorted, "All right, guys. Let's try the bastard . . ."

Schulze beamed around at the happy, flushed faces of the young, expectant troopers. Through the window outside, just back from Trier Station, Von Dodenburg paused too and watched. His heart went out to his teenage soldiers. Despite the brutalisation of their young lives by war, there was still something definitely innocent about them: all the whores, all the booze couldn't destroy that innocence. It would be the war itself that would destroy their spirit; turn them into old, crude, unfeeling automatons before their time – if they survived. His head said, 'They have to be tough'; his heart, on the contrary, pleaded, 'Let them live to become decent, honest, *ordinary* young men.' Their motto had to be: 'Not to die for Germany, but to live for it.'

"Now I shall start off with a couple of jokes," Schulze boomed. "Pay attention, jokes have to be taken seriously in Wotan or some of you will have the end of my dice-beaker" – he meant his great jackboot – "up yer fart-cannon." He cleared his throat and commenced the jokes they had all heard a dozen times before. "What does the man on leave say when he comes home to his old woman after six months at East Front?" He paused and prepared to deliver the punch line.

They beat him to it. A dozen voices yelled, "WHY, senior sergeant, he sez, 'Look at the ceiling, my beloved, 'cos you won't be seeing it for the next forty-eight hours' – and after that time, he takes off his pack. Ha, ha."

Schulze looked outraged. "Now how did you know that? Has some arse-with-ears been looking in my little black book, eh? Spit it out now."

However before Sergeant Schulze could act, he was disturbed by the sound of solemn church music coming from the anteroom. The door was opened. The duty corporal was standing there, looking flustered, "Sergeant Schulze . . . they're here . . ."

"Who man? . . . who? Piss or get off the pot . . ."

The words died on his lips, as a rotund figure in a red square hat, hands folded piously on his stomach, followed by a demure procession of nuns in great, white, flapping whimples, praying softly, entered, with a very girlish acolyte with plucked eyebrows and prettily rouged cheeks swinging incense from side to side.

"Frigging hell," one of the more inebriated troopers cursed in alarm, "it's the frigging Pope hissen."

Outside the window von Dodenburg gasped with surprise too. Where in three devils' name had this gang of motley papists come from, even in strictly Catholic Trier? For he did notice that most of the nuns, heads bent, as if in prayer, were wearing modish high heels, only obtainable on the black market.

"*Stehen,*" Schulze yelled in apparent surprise. "*Strammstehen . . . Der Herr Bischhof . . .*"

"Let us pray," the fat bishop said in one of those remote castrated voices of the high Roman clergy. Piously, his fat face shaded by his bishop's hat, he pressed his hands together in preparation for prayer, while the astonished troopers sprang to their feet, obviously wondering, von Dodenburg watching outside thought, what had hit them.

"*Nobis vic—*" the churchman commenced.

Surprisingly enough his nuns didn't seem to want to follow his example. Abruptly unseeming behaviour appeared to activate their black ranks. They raised their heads. They started tapping their feet. Fingers fumbled with their heavy robes. Von Dodenburg was sure he heard one of them curse, "Where's that frigging catch?" And in that same moment as the pious gramophone music from the anteroom was changed to that of the latest '*Yatz*', they'd whipped off their habits and to the amazed joy and delight of the young soldiers were rushing towards them, clad only in black stockings and high heels, squealing happily, their breasts bobbing up and down like newly released balloons.

"*Happy Christmas,*" Schulze cried, as Matz dropped his

cushions and other padding, grinning all over his wizened face as he grabbed the nearest whore's rather loose breast, clapped the nipple to his ear and yelled exuberantly, "I can't hear a bloody thing . . ."

"*No! . . . No! . . . No!*" Sergeant Rosenstein screamed, as Green Smoke released his grip and the 'court', which had sentenced him to death in less than sixty seconds, pushed him to the stinking, moving yellow pit. "NO! . . . PLEASE . . . NOT THAT . . ." His horror-contorted face turned a sickly green as he stared down, knowing what they intended. American kangaroo courts had done this before to prisoners they had regarded as traitors. It was the ideal way of carrying out an 'execution' without trace or firing squad. "I'll tell you everything . . . we're on the same side—" His words ended abruptly as someone whacked him squarely with the side of a plank.

Somehow he kept his balance, the blood streaming down from his smashed nose as he teetered on the edge of the pit. "Hit the bastard again!" Green Smoke commanded harshly.

Rosenstein grabbed frantically at the thin hessian. It ripped instantly. He staggered. The unknown whacked him again: a tremendous blow across the shoulders. Desperately he tried to keep his balance. For a brief moment it seemed he might do it. But no. Another blow sent him sprawling into the yellow mess. "That's it boys," Green Smoke urged. "We've got the Moxie bastard now!"

They dodged the nauseating stinking spray, as Rosenstein came up again, spluttering and choking and screaming, his eyes suddenly a brilliant white against the horrid yellow slime dribbling down his face. Feverishly he tried to claw his way out. Unintelligible, terrified sounds were bubbling out from his scummed, dripping lips. Swiftly, face brick-red with rage, as if he half-expected their victim to escape, Green Smoke grabbed the long-handled squeegee the fatigue men used to clean the place's duckboards.

He pushed Rosenstein under with a massive, enraged thrust.

He screamed. His breath was choked off as he disappeared again. A moment later he came up. His arm movements were slower now. He was tiring rapidly. Still he tried, his eyes bulging from his pathetic face like those of someone demented. Meaningless noises came from his lips, wide and gaping like those of a dying fish.

Green Smoke cursed. "For Chrissake, man – *die*!" he screamed and hit Rosenstein once more. The victim's head lolled to one side. His eyes clouded over. He started to sink. Obscene sucking, belching noises that the escaping air in his lungs made erupted as he did so.

Green Smoke stood there gasping frantically, squeegee held like a lance in his big, rough hands. But he needed it no more. Rosenstein was finished. The man who had planned for everything had not planned for this; the visionary, who had lived to create a new country for his oppressed people had never visualised that he would die like this: drowned in the shit of men who would never have been able to understand his vision even if he had told them.

For one long moment a pale hand surfaced, the fingers jerking convulsively. Then it too disappeared. For a moment or two the trapped air bubbles surfaced, to explode there obscenely. Then the surface of the evil yellow pit was without movement.

Major Gansenheimer was about finished. He had shinned up the two high poles the local Moselle fishermen used to hang their nets and had arranged the tow rope, plus the two blue lights. The poles weren't as high as the ones normally used by the Air Corps pickup planes, but they'd have to do. He had secured the approach from the road, the one he guessed any unwelcome visitors might use, littering it with the aptly named 'deballockers', tiny mines made from 45 cartridges which exploded and rose to waist-height with deadly effect on the victim's sexual future. Thereafter he had prepared the red signal light on the top of the Waco glider which he would ignite once the balloon had gone up.

Now, as calmly as if he were sitting back in the bar at the officers' club on base shooting the breeze with his fellow kid pilots, he smoked his cigar, every inch a 'Tiger', at peace with the world. Next to him in the cockpit there were his tommy-gun, extra 45 pistol, a thermite grenade in case he had to destroy the Waco, a couple of normal hand grenades and his escape pack, ready even down to the filled water-bottle (though he would have been forced to admit it didn't contain water, but straight bourbon; after all he *was* a 'Tiger', wasn't he?). He had his usual 'funnies' with him – he dearly loved 'Terry and the Pirates'. But the light was fading fast and he didn't want to strain his eyes unnecessarily. After all, he'd be flying most of the way back to the field at Châteaufontaine in darkness: a tough assignment in a plane without a motor.

Feet perched on the ledge in front of him, quietly puffing at his cigar, twenty-one-year-old Major Joseph Gansenheimer, soon to be recipient of the Congressional Medal of Honor, though he would never live long enough to receive it, waited patiently like a man with a whole world of time on his hands.

One by one the Marauders dropped to the ground. Over at the huts, the drunken prisoners had thrown open the doors of their huts – they had soon learned how to pick the locks. Weak yellow light streamed out onto the hard-packed white surface of snow. Here and there guards had yelled their protest. But they had done nothing. They were drunk themselves. Besides it was Christmas Eve. Next year, with luck they'd be civilians or prisoners of war themselves. What did it matter?

In the lead, Spiv positioned himself outside the admin block. He could hear the drunken Germans inside yelling and shouting above the dance music. Lucky sods, he said to himself. Nice and snug on a night like this. Then he gave an unholy smile. They weren't going to be nice and snug much longer.

Up in the guard tower, Mallory tensed behind the 'Hitler Saw', as the Hun soldiers called the machine gun which fired a thousand rounds a minute. Inside his head he ticked off the seconds. The light was almost gone in the west. They couldn't waste another second. He took a deep, controlled breath and pressed the trigger. The butt slammed into his shoulder painfully. At an amazing rate the belt of cartridges began to disappear into the breech. The air was suddenly full of the stench of tracer. Cartridge cases tumbled madly to the floor as the bullets arced across the camp to the guard tower at the opposite side of the hexagon. Woodwork splintered like matchwood. The guard screamed, flung up his arms melodramatically and pitched over the side, as the left leg of the tower started to crumple and the wooden edifice began to give way and fall.

Mallory dropped the gun. He grabbed the loud hailer. He had exactly five seconds before Kitchener cut off the generators and the power went. "Attention . . . attention . . ." he yelled urgently as the first plastic started to explode and great sections of the barbed wire flew apart, "this is the British Army . . . you're free . . . Go immediately to the exploded sections of the wire and make your way down the hill . . . Don't waste time . . . Attention . . . attention . . ." The sound went dead in the same instant that the lights cut and from the huts came a great drunken roar and burst of cheering, followed by a crazy rush of men, in all states of dress, for the doors.

Outside the headquarters block, Spiv no longer hesitated. He flung the grenade crying, "Try that on for frigging size, mate!" The .36 grenade exploded in an angry ball of fire and flying shrapnel. Next moment the plastic charges he had already planted started to explode. In an instant, the first wooden admin hut started to blaze furiously. Like tinderwood the next one caught light. A fat man without his trousers came screaming into the snow, waving his hand, yelling in German, "Save me, save me . . . I am *Kreisleiter—*" Schmeer never finished his cry for help as Spiv ran off into the lurid glowing gloom to help Thaelmann with the approaching truck. The flames welled up, their greedy scarlet fingers already tearing and plucking at his fat frame and he sank to the hissing, sizzling, blackening snow for good.

Up on the tower and with the others joining in as they ran back and forth completing their task of destruction, Mallory shouted for all he was worth, "Horowitz . . . Horowitz . . . General Horowitz, 82nd Airborne . . . rally on me . . . NOW!"

Obersturmbannführer Kuno von Dodenburg's harsh urgent command stopped the party dead. "*Achtung*!" he cried. "*Los zum Einsatz*! *Jetzt* . . . !"

Beer bottles were upset. Nuns, engaged in various sexual naughtiness in the shadows at the back of the room, screamed. 'Beer corpses', lying stiffly and apparently dead on couches, were resurrected by a swift kick of an NCO's boot and suddenly a drunken orgy had turned into an elite alarm company, surging out to battle.

"Christ on a crutch," Schulze gasped as he bolted outside, clutching his machine pistol like a child's toy in his mighty fist, "what a frigging Christmas Eve this is gonna be."

"Never fear, old house," Matz chortled, still half drunk and trying to discard his soutane as he hobbled to the waiting truck, "Jesus loves yer."

Wotan was going back to war.

ENVOI

"Poor young Gansenheimer bought the farm," General Horowitz said slowly and without pathos. He didn't even raise his voice as another flight of C-47s towing the troops of the British 6th Airborne and the US 17th Airborne across the Rhine appeared. The German flak on the eastern bank of Nazi Germany's last bastion took up the challenge. But their fire was much weaker now since the crossing.

"Yes, I've heard," Mallory answered, taking his gaze off Spiv and Kitchener who were looting the dead lying everywhere like bundles of abandoned rags. The term was unfamiliar, but he understood. "Brave young chap."

"Yeah. Brought his ship in totally ablaze and critically wounded. Still he landed us before he snuffed it. His CO says Ike" – he meant the Supreme Commander, Eisenhower – "has already agreed to have him recommended for the Congressional Medal." Horowitz, dark shadows under his eyes from the stress and strain of these last three months' planning for the great Anglo-American crossing of the Rhine, frowned.

"Penny for them?" Mallory said. He could see the top brass trying to restrain the 'former naval person' (as Churchill was code-named) from clambering up the bank on the eastern side of the Rhine.

Horowitz didn't look at him. His gaze was fixed on some horizon, distant and known only to him. "War is a waste, isn't it, Commander?"

Mallory didn't comment. It was a trite sentiment, often uttered, but he knew what the big Yank paratroop commander meant. "But still, General, we did what we intended to last December. A goodly few of your GIs made it to safety." He chuckled softly. "We even brought you back, though I must confess that my rogues would have much preferred their loot than generals."

Now General Horowitz chuckled, too. "Perhaps they were right as well. If more generals bought the farm then . . ." He didn't finish the sentence. At the bank, Churchill dressed in the uniform of a colonel in his old regiment, the 4th Hussars was waving his big cigar angrily and crying, "Let me die here while my blood's hot . . . It's the best way to die."

"Perhaps he's right," Mallory commented – to no one in particular.

Horowitz nodded simply. Perhaps he hadn't heard Mallory.

Some three hundred metres away, the fifty-odd survivors of SS Assault Regiment Wotan prepared to abandon their positions around the shattered windmill on the dominating height. The Amis had tried to take the place all night. Their dead bodies carpeted the hillside in solid khaki, stained with blood. Still they had not taken it. Soon they would withdraw a couple of hundred metres and let their artillery and air do the job for them before they attacked again with new troops. It was a typical old-fashioned Yankee tactic, von Dodenburg told himself. The Americans would never learn how really to fight a war.

It suited him personally. It would give his survivors time to withdraw safely, ordered as they had been by no less a person than *Reichsführer SS* Heinrich Himmler. Von Dodenburg had been informed by Corps HQ that their 'chief', knock-kneed, pale-faced weakling and time-server that he was, wanted them to be withdrawn and immediately reinforced. They were to be sent to Berchtesgaden, to the Führer's own 'Eagle's Nest', to defend it if the need arose. It was a great honour, von Dodenburg had been told.

One way or another he was unconcerned, save it would mean his survivors might live a few weeks longer. He supposed he owed his brave young men that. But in the end they'd all die violently, he knew that now. He felt bitter. After all they had been through, had fought and suffered, to die like this in some purposeless, last-ditch defensive position; while the fat, self-satisfied Amis with their jeeps and their tanks and their fancy rations—

"Fancy a snort, sir," Schulze broke into his angry silent reverie. "Got a flatman off'n one of the Ami stiffs. Silver too." He placed his sniper's rifle on the shell-churned earth and handed von Dodenburg the silver flask. "Go on, sir," he urged his beloved CO. "Plenty more where that came from. Them shitting rich Yanks have got everything. Sometimes I wonder why they come over here and start trouble in Europe when they've got so much back in their own frigging Homeland." He grabbed a drunken louse that was begin to stagger down from his sleeve. He ripped out its poor louse's life without noticing.

Von Dodenburg took a stiff drink while Schulze watched approvingly. Of late, he felt, the Old Man had been taking the war too seriously. "Enjoy the war, sir," he uttered the old phrase, "'cos peacetime's gonna be frigging awful."

Von Dodenburg finished his drink, wiped his skinny hand across his unshaven chin and commented, "I suppose you're right, you big rogue. But somehow . . . er . . ." – he groped for words – ". . . it ain't fair."

"When has life been fair, sir?" Schulze said easily and took the precious flask. "I'll get the lead out of the arses of those lame-tail ducks of ours, eh, sir?"

"Yes," von Dodenburg said absently. His gaze had suddenly fallen on two Amis, obviously officers, judging from the field glasses hanging from their chests, strolling across the battlefield to his immediate front like a pair of shitting tourists viewing some moderately exciting spectacle. "But leave your sniper's rifle, please."

Schulze seemed about to argue, then he changed his mind. "As you wish, sir. I'll have the greenbeaks ready to move off in ten minutes, sir."

"*Geht in Ordnung*," von Dodenburg answered absently, mind on other things.

He waited till Schulze had doubled away, ignoring the sudden irate tap-tap of an American machine gun and the tracer cutting the smoke-filled air in a lethal Morse. Then he picked up the rifle. He tested its balance. Excellent. Almost as if he was merely trying it out, he peered through the scope. He grunted. Again best German workmanship.

Zeiss probably. He put the stock to his right shoulder. He took his time adjusting the weapon snugly there.

Behind him Schulze was shouting his new orders. Like corpses ascending from the grave, the survivors of Wotan raised themselves from the foxholes the length of that lunar landscape. They blinked as if they were seeing light for the first time in many a year.

Everything seemed dreamlike. It all had a measured, unhurried pace. It was, von Dodenburg thought, as if he were watching an old, grainy film of only moderate interest, played in slow motion.

He heard himself click the bolt as the cartridge slid easily into the breech. He peered through the scope, only just aware that he was about to kill someone. A silent khaki shape slide into the circle of bright calibrated glass. Then another.

Above, a tiny Ami spotter plane had appeared from the other side of the Rhino. It was swooping and rising like a March lark, as if heralding the spring of 1945 now approaching. Von Dodenburg didn't notice it. Schulze did. It was an enemy artillery spotter plane. "Hurry, you idle dogs," he roared. "It's gonna be shitting steel soon!" Hastily he took another tremendous slug at his looted spirits and gasped. "Best part o' war," he choked to no one in particular, "in defeat there's allus plenty o' loot!"

Von Dodenburg didn't hear. He squinted down the barrel and into the scope. The two figures were stopped. They seemed deep in conversation, as if they didn't seem to realise that they were in the middle of a battlefield. "Supercilious swine," he whispered to himself. They thought they had won, the Ami bastards; that it was all over bar the shouting; contemptuous of the beaten Germans.

He controlled himself. The little plane had spotted them. A bright light was blinking off and on rapidly. It was signalling the artillery on the other side of the river. Soon the enemy guns would commence their work of destruction. It was time to go. But which one should he kill? He smiled momentarily, his lean death's-head face rapacious, lupine, predatory at the thought that he could at this minute decide how a man would die – and which one. God must feel like this, he told himself.

One wore a patch over his head. Perhaps his eye had been shot out. He would be worthless in a fighting unit with one eye. Perhaps he was staff. The other, who wore a helmet was dark and powerful. He looked like a soldier in his trim uniform and high boots, breast heavy with medal ribbons . . . a real fighting soldier. He would be the one.

Behind him, Schulze shrilled three blasts on his whistle. He was standing bolt upright, regardless of the impending danger, silhouetted against the drifting smoke of battle. "*Los*!" he yelled, half drunk by now. "Come on, you sacks . . . the captain has a hole in his arse – FOLLOW ME. Laughing uproariously, waving his silver flask, he staggered down the churned-up mound followed by his survivors.

Von Dodenburg only half heard. What did it matter? What did anything matter? For a brief moment he would play God and then – he pressed the trigger, hardly aware that he had done so. The rifle thumped back into his shoulder. His nostrils were assailed by the stink of burned cordite. A couple of hundred yards away, Brigadier-General Moses Horowitz, late of the 'All Americans' of the US 82nd Airborne Division, started to crumple to the ground.

NOTE

Gentle Reader, if you have enjoyed reading this new Wotan adventure, look out for the next one, *The Battle for Hitler's Eagle's Nest* by Leo Kessler.